D0197528

LIFE AFTER
DIVORCE
A SINGLE MOTHER'S GUIDE

JIM TALLEY
with
LESLIE H. STOBBE

NAVPRESS ◐

A MINISTRY OF THE NAVIGATORS
P.O. BOX 35001, COLORADO SPRINGS, COLORADO 80935

The Navigators is an international Christian organization.
Jesus Christ gave His followers the Great Commission to
go and make disciples (Matthew 28:19). The aim of The
Navigators is to help fulfill that commission by multiply-
ing laborers for Christ in every nation.

NavPress is the publishing ministry of The Navigators.
NavPress publications are tools to help Christians grow.
Although publications alone cannot make disciples
or change lives, they can help believers learn biblical
discipleship, and apply what they learn to their lives and
ministries.

Cover illustration: Warren Gebert

Special acknowledgment is made to Richard Church,
President of FYI Statistical Research, Modesto, California,
for the statistical data taken from the Dialog Information
Services. CENDATA was the source for Census Bureau
Survey information.

All of the names of persons mentioned throughout this
book have been changed, unless they are quoted in pub-
lished material or referenced as recommended sources.

Unless otherwise identified, all Scripture in this publica-
tion is from the *New American Standard Bible* (NASB), © The
Lockman Foundation 1960, 1962, 1963, 1968, 1971, 1972,
1973, 1975, 1977. Another version used is the *Holy Bible:
New International Version* (NIV). Copyright © 1973, 1978,
1984, International Bible Society. Used by permission of
Zondervan Bible Publishers.

Printed in the United States of America

FOR A FREE CATALOG OF
NAVPRESS BOOKS & BIBLE STUDIES,
CALL TOLL FREE 1-800-366-7788 (USA)
or 1-416-499-4615 (CANADA)

Contents

To
my mother, Mrs. Murdice Talley,
one example of the principles
of this book
in that she chose not to remarry
while her children were at home.

Preface

One of the questions I'm frequently asked is, "Why should you write a book for single mothers — what do *you* know?"

For me, the concern for single parenting started in my own childhood. As the oldest of four children raised by a single mother, I was forced to face life's big issues at a young age. At age twelve I had to share the responsibility of parenting, and for the next seven years the issues of children and parenting were with me every day.

I feel that having to assist in the parenting role in my family brought me a tremendous amount of maturity and responsibility. For most twelve-year-olds, the realities of daily living can be very vague. But they were very clear and immediate for me as I cared for my three younger siblings.

The skills I learned during those early years have shaped my character to this day. A deep concern for other people has become a primary issue in my life. Acquiring this concern early in life, while assisting my own family, has allowed me to achieve some unique levels of personal ministry.

My heart has always been moved by the children of single parents. The past twenty years of my current ministry have been focused on providing the ministry and support necessary to meet the needs of single-parent families.

Joyce and I were married in 1961, and we have shared this calling to singles and their children in a variety of settings. Since 1976 we have worked specifically in the area of single adults and their children. The principles and stories in this book come from our experiences with thousands of single parents in the day-to-day reality of ministry, not just from research into parenting theory.

I am grateful for the assistance of Les Stobbe in writing the manuscript for this book. Les and I have worked together on several projects, and we share the same concern for ministry and the needs of people. Les and his wife, Rita, have given themselves in service to many people over the years. Some of the stories in this book also reflect the experiences of Les and Rita in their work with single parents.

The stories in this book are true, although the names have been changed. The principles I share are valuable because they come from the Word of God. My purpose has been to share the experiences of others—good and bad—so that correct choices can be made and mistakes avoided.

ONE

It's Not Easy Being a Single Parent

Some people say that life begins at thirty. For me, life began at age twelve.

That was the year when my dad walked out on the five of us and never came back. It was also the year I was arrested for shoplifting and spent a day in jail.

But not everything in my life was a disaster. The tiny church we attended rallied around my mom and us four kids. And best of all, I made a personal commitment to Jesus Christ, a commitment that ultimately led me into a profession where I can help single parents get the same kind of help my mom got.

My family were migrant farm workers, following the harvest season by season as we traveled Route 66 between Oklahoma and central California. Just before my fateful twelfth year my dad failed in a small business venture, triggering a year of conflict and physical abuse . . . and ultimately his departure.

Suddenly I was the man of the house, helping to look after a seven-year-old, a five-year-old, and a three-year-old. Fortunately, we had begun to attend a migrant camp church supported by the Missionary Gospel Fellowship in Shafter, California.

From the moment I put my faith in Jesus Christ I knew I would serve Him the rest of my life — probably as a pastor. But first I had to help my mom survive as a single parent. With the church's help we made it through the first year. Then my mother enrolled in a Licensed Vocational Nursing program. For the next two years we survived on welfare payments and church help until she finished her courses and could get a job that paid more than minimum wage.

This experience shaped my future involvement with singles, for I learned firsthand what so many single parents need even today to survive until they can get back on their feet: *financial assistance, spiritual and emotional support,* and *training* so they can find a skilled position that pays a living wage.

By the time I was nineteen, mom was able to function on her own. In 1961, I married Joyce Burr, and we began our own family.

Along my educational path I stopped just short of an engineering degree and instead went into a street ministry in Modesto, California. As a way to gain financial support and supply jobs for that ministry I studied for and gained a license as a general building contractor while I worked as a computer operator for a major construction company. I'm a living example that the oldest son in a single-parent family can make it and be successful.

In the mid-seventies the Lord opened the door for me to work with single adults when I became singles pastor at what is now the largest church in Modesto. My computer files hold the names of over ten thousand singles we have ministered to, as well as more than four thousand single parents I have counseled individually over the last twenty years. Today I average over four hundred phone calls a month with singles, while counseling six to eight single parents each week in my office.

LEARNING FROM OTHERS

So, even though I'm not a single mom, and even though every person's pain is uniquely her own, I think I have some idea where you're coming from, how you feel, and what you fear the most.

If I'm right, I'd guess that your number one fear is that *you won't be able to raise your children, and especially your sons*—right? If I guessed correctly, you can be sure you're not alone. Thousands of women have told me that this is what they fear most. As you read this material you will notice I'm always aware of that fear.

Some of you may struggle with other fears, such as support, spousal relations, child visitation, financial survival, or even another father for your children.

In the coming chapters we will focus together on an issue you can't deny: you are a *single* parent. Yes; the father of your children may still live in your community. But through signing the divorce papers (possibly against your wishes) and listening to the pronouncement of a judge, you became a single parent.

If you're like so many women I've counseled, what your heart is experiencing each morning is not the exhilaration of standing on a beautiful hilltop looking excitedly ahead to the future. Instead, you feel as though your feet are stuck in the mud at the bottom of a brushy, dark valley.

More than anything you just want desperately to climb to higher ground. How can you avoid the flash flood of negative emotion that threatens to engulf your life? All you want to be, for the sake of your kids, is the best single parent possible.

YOU CAN'T GO IT ALONE

This probably will not come as a surprise, but before you can reach high ground, you will have to scramble through a boulder-filled valley. Life isn't easy for anyone, and certainly not for single parents. Yet my mom, and many others I have counseled, testify that "you can make it." They have experienced that you'll meet God in the valley just as much as you'll see Him on the mountaintop.

The last thing you need now are quick fixes, or promises that remain just that . . . promises. What you *really* need is reality—tough as it may seem at the time. But the reality must be tinged with the rainbow of hope.

The hard truth you must accept is that *you can't go it alone.* No, I'm not suggesting you make a permanent reservation at the nearest counseling center. Nor do I suggest you drop everything and rush into a new relationship. I am suggesting that God can provide resources that, when properly utilized, will help you not only make it as a single parent, but also provide the foundation for your child's successful entry into adulthood. An exciting possibility is that *your need to depend on God may even make you into a better parent than if your ex were still parenting with you.*

HARD? YES—IMPOSSIBLE? NO

A recent book by Judith Wallerstein and Sandra Blakeslee, *Second Chances: Men, Women and Children a Decade After a Divorce,* reveals some startling research results about children raised in single-parent homes:

- Half of the children studied grew up in families where the parents stayed angry at each other even after divorce.
- Three out of five kids felt rejected by at least one of the parents.
- Half became worried, underachieving, insecure, and sometimes angry young adults.
- Of the children who witnessed violence between their parents (but were not themselves abused), half entered abusive relationships as adults.
- For daughters, the entry into adulthood is much harder than for sons because that's when relationships and career choices move onto center stage—and girls seem to have a lot more trouble in relationships with the opposite sex.
- Young women are often drawn to older men to fill the father void.
- For young men there is a tremendous tension between what they want—commitment and lasting love—and what they expect. As a result, sons raised in single-parent families tend to drift, with few having lasting relationships with women.[1]

Given this scenario, what should a single mom do? Move quickly into another relationship so the kids will feel part of a whole family? Authors Wallerstein and Blakeslee reveal this is not a good solution either, for "half [of the children] saw one parent get a second divorce within ten years of the first one."[2] One divorce is bad enough; the second is often more devastating.

Is the situation hopeless? Not at all, say these researchers: "A whole lot of these young people do succeed. . . . These stages of life are harder. They are not impossible."[3]

WHAT THIS BOOK WILL OFFER YOU

In the face of discouragement, there *is* hope. To acquaint you with what's ahead, here's an overview of the ideas I'll be developing in this book:

- During the early months after the divorce, it is more important to focus on getting yourself together rather than on your role as a single parent.
- Your goal should be not just to raise your children to be healthy, well-rounded adults, but for them to become good parents themselves.
- Good instruction on how to grow up and become a good parent is not restricted to the two-parent family. A child can learn good parenting skills from a single parent.
- Eighty percent of all parenting functions can be performed by one parent—and the rest can usually be gained from family members, friends, and other church members.
- Too much change will not only result in mental instability, but also break the good peer relationships the children may have developed. Moving children around can destroy their social stability.
- Reaching a point where you can say, "I can be civil with my ex" will not only help keep child-support flowing but also provide the father-child relationships so vital to the healthy development of children.
- Finally, throughout the book we'll explore a question you may have asked yourself but were afraid to answer: "Should I consider staying single until my children are grown?"

TAKE TIME TO RECOVER

The most devastating thing you can do is to attempt to go through the recovery process too rapidly. Speed produces relapses. Healing and returning to normalcy take time. "Time is your ally, not your enemy," it's been said. This is true for the single parent.

I sometimes compare becoming a single parent after a divorce to a marathon runner who has to have open heart surgery. The marathoner will be up and walking in a few days. But she will probably need most of a year before she can do intensive physical activity, two to three years to do any heavy training, and possibly four to five years to run a competitive marathon. If the marathoner rushes the process, she will experience one relapse after another, perhaps even serious damage requiring an even longer recovery period.

It's the same with the single parent. The most common mistake is expecting too short a recovery time. If you move too fast through each stage, you run the risk of continually failing and becoming more and more discouraged. Paradoxically, the more discouraged we get, the more desperate we get, and the faster we go to try to recover—a cycle that takes us down deeper and deeper into the emotional pit of despair.

RECOGNIZE THAT CHANGE IS STRESSFUL

The reality you face as you seek recovery typically follows a pattern like the "change curve" in figure 1 (page 16).

You might think that the movement from Point A to Point B in divorce recovery would progress smoothly upward from one level to the next. *But things always get worse before they get better.* Let me explain.

Figure 1
Change Curve

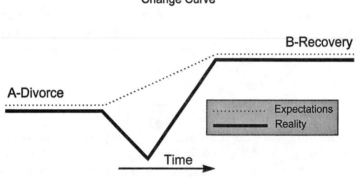

Suppose you were being beaten and generally abused in your marriage. You decide to go from Point A to Point B and get out of the relationship. So you launch off into the change—the divorce and single parenting. Before moving you are convinced you will be a lot better off—spiritually, emotionally, lovingly, and financially.

But then your expectations meet reality. Instead of improving, after the change you find yourself *slipping* down the line of reality. One reason why this is so hard to understand is that you *do* feel relief because of the divorce. But instead of progressing straight up toward Point B, you slide down spiritually, emotionally, lovingly, and financially before you begin to recover.

One troubling example of this "slipping down" experience for many new single parents is the drastic decline in financial resources. The Census Bureau reports that family income drops 37 percent within four months of separation.[4] This can mean everything from mild disaster to bankruptcy. (Later in this book I will provide you with numerous suggestions on how to tackle this decline.)

The next notch on the downward slide is the need for a father image. Especially if you have sons, you may feel the need to be sure they get a father image soon—after all, according to our culture, sons need fathers, don't they? Yes, they do, but there are other solutions instead of remarriage. Just finding a father is not something you want to rush into, for reasons I will explain fully in this book. But let me give just one scenario.

A woman in our church was widowed after four children had arrived. She quickly tried to get into another relationship for the sake of the children. When she could not find a man in the church, she began dating outside of the church and in the process became pregnant. Since she was opposed to abortion, she now had five children. Several more relationships later she finally said, "Hey, I have enough to do in my life. I'm going to stay single."

This woman stayed single for eighteen years, with the last child just finishing high school, when Mr. Right arrived on the scene. She is now happily married and doing extremely well. She did not marry for the children's sake, but for a relationship that can get better as she gets older—because she married to gain a husband, not a father.

GOD'S PROMISE TO THE FATHERLESS

One of the most reassuring things I can say to a single mom is that *God pays special attention to the widowed and fatherless*. Scripture makes it very clear that He wants to take care of you! His admonition to the church in James 1:27 is just one example: "This is pure and undefiled religion in the sight of our God and Father, to visit orphans and widows in their distress, and to keep oneself unstained by the world."

Psalm 146:9 provides another example: "The LORD protects the strangers; He supports the fatherless and the widow." Repeatedly in Isaiah (see 1:17, 1:23), God makes it plain that one element in regaining His favor is for rulers to take care of the orphan and the widow. Single mom, *God sees your needs and the needs of your children and He is on your side.*

If you're like the single parents I know, you are sincerely searching for an objective view of life and a plan for progress. You want to gain control of yourself, achieve a measure of objectivity about your experience, turn from looking backward to looking forward, and begin to take charge of your life.

One important step in this plan is to *find a church.* Check with other single parents and find a strong Bible-teaching church to attend. Once you're there, *stay!* Don't be a church-hopper and drag your children from one youth group to another. The Lord desires to bless you and fill your life with hope as you continue to serve Him.

SUMMARY

It's not easy being a single parent. But you can minimize the difficulties with these principles:

Accept the fact that you are not alone: God is with you.

Reset your expectations for recovery: time is your ally, not your enemy.

Limit changes in your life to gain emotional stability.

Remember: Before you can climb the mountain you will go through the valley. But it's not impossible, especially if the God who owns the valley is leading you through it.

TWO

Understanding the Agony

W hy is divorce is one of the most devastating events in the life of a human being?

Let's compare it to another horrible experience— imprisonment. If you were a prisoner of war or detained in a slave labor camp, you would know your torture was being administered by people who hated you or just saw you as a number. But in divorce, the pain is inflicted by a person who once claimed he loved you. That really hurts.

Now, you might answer me, "Divorce can't be any worse than the emotional and physical wringer I went through during my marriage. I'm *glad* I'm out from under the abuse of that beast."

Granted, the emotional roller coaster of your marriage before separation and divorce was awful. But those emotional storms probably will get worse before they get better because you may not yet have experienced the full impact of *alienation*.

What is alienation? The best definition I've found was in an unpublished article by Eugene McCreary entitled "Alienation":

It is the name for a weakening of the ties of community and family, for the loss of creative enjoyment in work, for uncertainty in all things, for
dependency and the confusing and contradic-
tory expectations of economic and social life,
for weakened personal integrity, for a sense of
hopelessness, meaninglessness, uselessness, and
irrelevance, for conformity in culture and politics,
for a loss of faith, for the separation of man from
his natural roots, for the decay of love. The alienated are unable to realize or define themselves. The
dimensions of alienation are a generalized anxiety,
shifting from object to object, and a confused and
debilitated sense of human identity and personal
responsibility. The alienated stand as ready pawns
for strange new faiths, for excitements strong
enough to divert them, for cruel myths of polarized
evil and virtue, and for a shifting of responsibility
to others.[1]

Many recently divorced single parents have told me,
"Wow, that really describes how I feel." One woman
said, "Every morning after our separation I was sorry I
woke up. I felt like going into a corner and just dying. But
I knew I couldn't do that because I had two daughters to
care for."

Others have described the alienation experience as
"spinning on the inside and unable to stop." The spinning never seems to stop, not even when they try to go to
sleep. It is the equivalent of being on an amphetamine, of
having a chemical rush. In alienation everything speeds
up in your life . . . and you cannot stop it. So you use up
all your energy coping with how you feel — you can't even
think clearly.

Sometimes, if the marriage was short, with no property or children, there is a reduced reaction to alienation. But nearly every break in a significant relationship causes this painful condition to some degree.

HOW MARRIAGES DIE

How did you end up where your are? Chances are your marriage began to die long before "everything fell apart." If you and your spouse were not actively "cultivating" the garden of your marriage, the weeds were coming up and eventually took over. This disunion probably was very subtle, maybe not even noticeable for months. But it was there, and it moved forward with the slow but steady pace of a glacier.

Time Runs Out

Consider the relationship between Wagner and Lisa. Their families had known each other for years. Wagner and Lisa went to the same grade school, junior high school, high school, junior college, and college. They found themselves together at various occasions, but there was no romantic attachment.

In college Wagner began to see Lisa through the other guys' eyes. She was witty, intelligent, beautiful. Soon Wagner and Lisa were spending late nights studying together. This led to premarital sex, but they justified it by saying they planned to get married right after graduation. Lisa would have her RN and work to put Wagner through graduate school.

All went according to plan, and Wagner and Lisa were married. After the honeymoon Lisa went to work at the hospital and Wagner hit the books. They began their life together—except it was more apart than together now.

Their separate schedules were very busy and all that time they had spent together before marriage developing their friendship and relationship was just a pleasant memory. Time was running out.

Disunion began to take its toll on their marriage. Just as Wagner was about to graduate with his master's degree, they realized the relationship had gone full circle. All they had in common now was a marriage license and a king-sized bed.

One of the principles I developed in an earlier book, *Too Close, Too Soon*,[2] is that in the development of a relationship, a man and a woman first establish friendship, then move to a relationship, which is defined as doing anything with the opposite sex you would not do with the same sex.

This is what had happened to Wagner and Lisa. They had moved from friendship to a relationship, to emotional togetherness, to sexual intimacy in their marriage—and then they drifted back down through the stages to only occasional physical involvement.

Suddenly they realized they were again only friends. Without commitment they really had no glue in their marriage. So instead of re-committing themselves to each other, they shook hands and got a divorce. They provided an example of the principle that Dr. William E. Yaeger has stated, "the normal direction of a marriage is to separate!"

If Wagner had paid as much attention to his relationship as he did to his car—which he serviced faithfully, washed regularly, and protected from the elements—he would probably still be married. Instead, his marriage deteriorated at a faster rate than his car, because he did not understand the truth that *time alone together builds a relationship*. Since Lisa and Wagner had experienced most of life independent of the other, their marriage's slow death began shortly after the honeymoon. And because their marriage had never had a high degree of emotional intimacy, their divorce produced a minimal amount of alienation.

Conflict Remains Unresolved

Judy and Philip present a contrast to Lisa and Wagner. They had dated steadily through high school and were always the life of the party. Yet that was not the real "face" for this relationship, since they experienced a regular cycle of fighting and making up, at which point they usually ended up in bed. After this went on for two years, six months on and six months off, they finally said, "Let's get married."

Marriage did not prove to be a magic solution. Now when they fought, they found they were married and had nowhere to go to cool off. Philip worked in a garage and put in long hours, especially after a fight with Judy. But his good wages made it possible for Judy to pursue her own interests: volunteer work at a medical center, racquetball twice a week, exercise classes. Since she did not care for housework she, according to Philip, let the home "go to pot."

Philip and Judy had not dealt successfully with their anger before their marriage or during their marriage. So they walked down the steps of deterioration (see figure 2 on the following page), which can lead from anger to bitterness to pugnaciousness (meaning aggressive, or eager to fight) and even to physical death. In this case the alienation was severe, since Philip and Judy both blamed each other for their inability to make a go of it in marriage. After reaching the pugnacious level they divorced.

Figure 2
Steps of Destruction

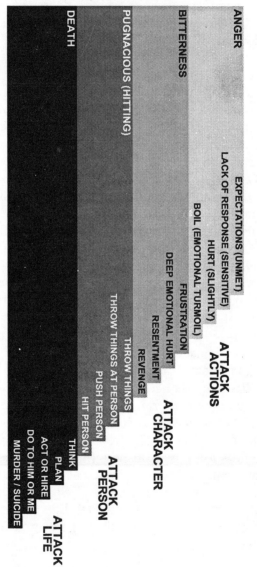

Someone Goes Outside the Marriage

Clark and Susan represent another type of couple I often encounter. Clark's father was a minister who controlled his family to the point of telling them what kind of clothing to wear. Clark resented this control and began leading a double life, which he brought with him into marriage. Three years into the marriage, while he was teaching a Bible class and giving the appearance of a devout and devoted husband, he had an affair.

Clark told Susan he was sorry, and she believed his assurances that this had been a brief fling and would not happen again.

Some time later Clark asked Susan not to work. She agreed and happily helped him with his homework while he gained his master's degree. When he wanted to move onto a ranch with friends in Minnesota, she went willingly. They had been there only nine months when Susan discovered he was having another affair.

Confronted, Clark suggested they have an open marriage in which he could date and she could as well. Devastated, Susan sought support from her friends and got none. "I felt like I had been knocked down on the floor by them and walked on. I felt totally abandoned, thousands of miles from any family," she confessed. Her telephone bill skyrocketed as she talked with her parents and the pastor of the church back home.

She soon left Clark and with her two girls moved back into her parents' home in a southeastern city. Her mother helped her get a job and within a year Susan joined her sister in a trek to California, where she found another job.

Clark, however, did not give up. For the next twelve months he called every week to urge her to return, assuring her that he had changed, that he had left his immoral life behind. She finally moved to Minnesota to be with

Clark, and even though their divorce was not yet final, they had a lovely remarriage ceremony.

For three months everything seemed to go well. Then Clark reverted to his old habits—the easy come, easy go syndrome. The easier it is for a person like Clark to come back into the house, the easier it is for him to leave. If you can convince him to get into a counseling program before you rejoin him you have a chance, though even then there are dangers, as Susan was to discover.

Susan insisted that they should have marriage counseling once she saw what was happening, and he agreed. But instead of attempting to find a solution, Clark insisted he was attracted to other women because his wife was so unattractive.

"At the counseling sessions together he repeatedly called me ugly, that he hated the way my skin looked, that I was completely unattractive to him," says Susan.

Unwilling to continue taking the abuse, Susan dropped out of counseling after three sessions. Then Clark dropped out. Susan contacted the counselor, and he helped her get a lawyer with a contact in California. Susan again moved back to California with the children, only this time she felt doubly devastated.

"I would wake up at night totally bathed in sweat. I felt ugly, unwanted, and unworthy of anyone's love," says Susan. This appears to be the bottom for Susan, but later on we'll learn the rest of the story. Our God is a God of hope! Even in the midst of alienation God can do exciting things in our lives.

HOW ALIENATION KNOCKS US OFF BALANCE

After personally counseling thousands of divorced men and women, I have reached the conclusion that alienation is one of the most excruciating things that can happen to a human being. Illness, such as a serious heart attack or paralysis, can be devastating physically but does not necessarily handicap us totally in every area. But in divorce the alienation can consume so much of our emotional energy that we can't even think straight or function in a normal fashion.

For an illustration of this energy distribution, examine the circle diagrams in figure 3 (pages 28-29). The larger the circle, the greater the energy reservoir. Low-energy people have a smaller circle. Each quarter represents an area of our life that consumes energy: physical, emotional, spiritual, mental.

Ideally, we should be rather balanced. If we do hard work we use up a lot of our physical energy, some emotional energy, some spiritual energy, and some mental energy. If we balance our checkbook we use up a greater amount of mental energy, considerable emotional energy, some physical energy, and a little spiritual energy. But our reservoirs rapidly return to a normal 25 percent balanced state.

When a couple divorces, each of the spouses typically experiences such total emotional alienation that I estimate they each consume around 85 percent of their energy trying to deal with their emotional upheaval. This leaves only 15 percent for the other three categories: 5 percent mental energy, 5 percent physical energy, and 5 percent spiritual energy.

People describe this emotional drain in a variety of ways, but what it boils down to is that the emotional drain almost totally engages the person. This is particularly true if you are a single parent, for now you not only have to deal with your own needs but with those of the children as well.

Figure 3
Five years to complete the cycle

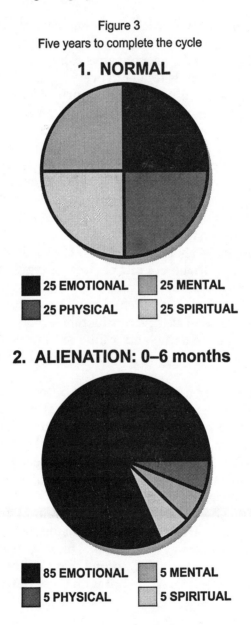

1. NORMAL

25 EMOTIONAL	25 MENTAL
25 PHYSICAL	25 SPIRITUAL

2. ALIENATION: 0–6 months

85 EMOTIONAL	5 MENTAL
5 PHYSICAL	5 SPIRITUAL

3. RECOVERY: 6 months–2 years

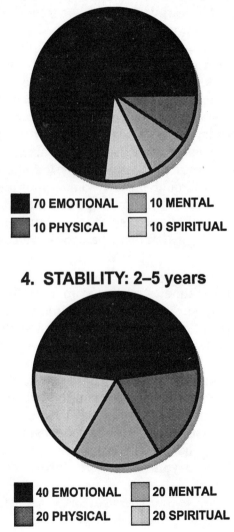

70 EMOTIONAL   10 MENTAL

10 PHYSICAL   10 SPIRITUAL

4. STABILITY: 2–5 years

40 EMOTIONAL   20 MENTAL

20 PHYSICAL   20 SPIRITUAL

Mental Energy Is Depleted

Thus it's not surprising to learn that when you're caught up in divorce you're in short supply of a crucial ingredient you need in order to understand what is happening to you: mental energy. You find it extremely difficult to mentally process what has happened. Someone says to you, "Here, read this book. It's so helpful." You take it home, read two sentences, and put it down—unable to concentrate even though you may have an insatiable appetite for understanding what has happened.

A hospital stay provides a good comparison. How many times have people taken books to the hospital and never even opened them? The pain and disorientation of a hospital stay requires all of your physical energy just for you to make it through the day, so now your resources are divided as 70 percent physical, 10 percent mental, 10 percent emotional, and 10 percent spiritual. For most of us, there isn't enough energy left to read a book—even the Bible.

Recovery Time Slows

Just as it takes time to recover from a stay in the hospital, especially surgery, so it takes time to recover from the emotional "open heart" surgery of the alienation in divorce. The first indication of recovery is that your mind finally begins to clear. You can read a whole chapter of a book in one sitting. You aren't constantly misplacing your keys. You can even "balance" your checkbook to within twenty dollars! Progress: ah, sweet progress!

After about one or two years you sense that you really are recovering, but the downside is that you also realize how unbalanced you really were during the depths of your alienation.

After three to four years you may pass the 50 percent mark, so that less than half of your energy is used for emotions, freeing up the other half for mental (17 percent), physical (16 percent), and spiritual (17 percent) purposes. Recovery: ah, sweet recovery!

The better you get, the clearer it becomes how far down you really were. Matt, a professor of English, can remember students in his classes six to seven years before his divorce and every year since. But when students approach him from the year of his divorce, he cannot remember even one. He was a walking, talking zombie who did his job by robotic instinct.

In my counseling I warn single parents that it takes a full five years from the divorce date to recover from such intense emotional alienation. When I say this I can almost hear their hearts hit the ground. They don't want to believe it, but I have seen it over and over again. Wallerstein and others have studied the long-term impact of divorce on children and parents. These studies show that many times even fifteen years later the issues are still unresolved. So understanding what is really happening during the divorce process is critical to recovery.

RELATIONSHIPS:
THE ATTEMPTED SHORTCUT TO RECOVERY

What takes away pain in the hospital? Addictive pain killers. What takes away the pain in divorce? Often, *addictive physical relationships*. These can become the novocaine of the heart. Many divorced persons are so relieved to be out of an abusive or lonely marriage that they immediately embark on a new relationship.

One woman I counseled told me that she had gone through seventeen sexual relationships in less than a year after her divorce. She is not all that atypical, even for Christians and members of the church. Remember, she has only 5 percent of spiritual energy.

I frequently find people already dating during the separation period prior to divorce. Although they know they shouldn't, a lot of separated Christians date. Many more start right after the divorce is final. This can be a tragic mistake.

Remember the energy circles? Typically, a recently divorced person has only 5 percent of her mental capacity to sort things out, because 85 percent of the energy is being burned up emotionally. Often, this means she's not paying much attention to the character or moral qualities of the person she's dating. She doesn't have the mental energy to be objective. All the divorced person deeply desires is a relationship that can anesthetize the pain. But just as running on a broken foot with pain killers increases damage to the injury, so dating with a broken heart can actually increase damage to the already injured heart.

In this situation, dating may lead to marriage, but not necessarily to recovery. This is one reason why so many second marriages fail. The dating usually ends in a marriage to someone who would not be considered if the person were in her "right mind" — with the normal 25 percent of mental energy and decision-making abilities. And as incredible as it may seem, this someone she marries is usually just like her ex.

We tend to gravitate toward people who are familiar to us, people we're comfortable with. Alcoholics Anonymous and Alanon are examples of programs where people often meet and then marry a series of partners who have similar problems. We tend to marry the kind of people we associate with. As a result the second marriage fails for the same reasons the first one failed.

The breakup of the second marriage increases the emotional trauma and alienation. Now after this second "mistake" comes intense anger at both first and second spouses.

People whose second marriage dissolves have an additional issue. The first time around they blame their mate, or at worst say it was a fifty-fifty proposition. But now there is only one common denominator in the first and second failure . . . themselves. Waves of self-hatred may threaten to drown them, and now the spiral downward to deep discouragement and even depression really accelerates. They are reset to the 85 percent emotional circle, and the cycle repeats itself.

In our society there is a new development in mental health care—short-term care for divorced persons with extreme alienation. Some people in this extreme condition wouldn't even have the energy to pick up this book. They're just worn out.

Singles experiencing this condition often go into what I call emotional free fall by cutting themselves off from all of their natural support systems. When the fighting started in their marriage they didn't want their parents to know, so they stopped going to family celebrations. Likewise, they may not have let their children go to the grandparents because they knew the kids would talk.

Single parents in this state are often too embarrassed to talk about the marital woes at church or on the job, so emotional ties are cut there too. They try to go it alone, not having the mental energy to know they won't be able to do that. They continue the total isolation until the divorce is final.

If you enjoy keeping a diary, using a prayer journal, or just recording your experiences, you may be able to use this as a way to pour out to God your feelings of anger and alienation during this period. But don't be surprised if you lack energy to do this in the beginning.

Single people in emotional free fall are very vulnerable. Unscrupulus dating services may prey on these people, abounding with smooth talkers who provide a semblance of emotional support for the sole purpose of victimizing the single person financially and even sexually. A recent story on the program *America's Most Wanted* centered on a man who robbed and killed a woman he met and married through a dating service.

Incredible as it may seem, the devastation of this alienation, of the emotional free fall, can overpower the strongest parenting instinct. Many single dads and some single moms have even abandoned their children to deal with their own emotional hurt. The mother may spend more money than she should on clothes so she will look nice for a date; meanwhile her kids go hungry. One woman left her two small babies and ran off with her lover. She didn't even try to see her children for ten years.

For people in this emotional free fall, cut off from people of faith and their parents or other family, a dating relationship can appear to be the most pleasurable, anesthetic, pain-relieving experience imaginable. Is it any wonder a hurting woman may unwittingly ignore her children? She may tell me, "I've just had the most enjoyable time! I've been with a man who brought me flowers, paid for my dinner, and gave me a gift. I haven't been treated this well for fifteen years. You want me to stop, Jim? Forget it!"

Many times I've had to get firm with such single moms. Their kids may be underfed and wearing ragged clothing because the pain of the alienation is so intense — in this extreme form it can last for several months. The parenting role then typically falls to the oldest child because the child has more mental energy than the parent. The children have now "lost" both parents and have to become "little adults" to survive.

Some single moms who are experiencing severe emotional pain look desperately for a relationship—*any* relationship. Often they attract the wrong type: an alcoholic, a drug user, or a people user. Many of the domestic calls to police departments are about abusive live-in partners.

If you're recently divorced, please recognize how vulnerable you are. These men may take your money, have sex with you, and just plain live off you—leaving you with nothing for taking care of your children. Are these men really out there? Just look in your local paper under personal ads.

This sad turn of events can happen to a Christian woman just as easily as to a nonChristian. (Perhaps this is the situation the Apostle Paul described in 2 Timothy 3:2-7 when he referred to men who prey on "weak-willed women"—verse 6, NIV.) In fact, some people suffering from alienation may run from their faith. Once the separation has happened, and certainly by the time the divorce is final, the person may leave the church and take the children along.

Some people have a different experience. If they haven't been attending church, the pain of alienation may be so intense it actually drives them *into* the church. Agony can be spiritually invigorating.

Many churches want to minister to the family, but a divorced woman may be viewed as "dangerous" by married couples. One woman I counseled said, "I felt like I ought to put a sign on my back at church that said, 'I don't want your man.'"

At our church I see a constant flow of single parents who have not set foot in a church for ten to fifteen years. The pain of alienation has become so excruciating that not even alcohol, drugs, or sex can defeat it. They come to church because at one time they found help there—or their parents did. They are ready to learn more about a Savior who loves them unconditionally, who is a support system all by Himself. Jesus won't abuse them or their children or become a leech on the family. He is trustworthy in all of life's situations.

SUMMARY

Remember these principles in understanding the agony:

Be aware of how alienation impacts your life.

Realize that the normal direction of a marriage is to separate.

Recognize that agony can be spiritually invigorating.

Every new single parent is looking for a stabilizer. In the next chapter we will examine faulty stabilizers, but also see the true Stabilizer, the One who can make a huge difference in you and the life of your children.

THREE

Stabilizing Life After Divorce

Picture yourself in a sailboat out on a lake or at sea. What do you do when a squall comes up? You batten down the hatches, turn into the wind, and do whatever is necessary to stabilize the boat. And then you hang on tight.

That's also what we do in life when important relationships run into a squall. And sometimes those squalls come totally unexpected.

"I was totally complacent in our marriage," recalled Ginger. "I was moderately satisfied as a stay-at-home mother of two boys with a husband able to support us. In reality I was totally out of touch, especially with what was going on in my husband's life. Then one day my husband announced that he was moving out, that I could have the children.

"I had gotten so complacent I didn't even realize I had any emotions left. But when my husband told me he was moving out it was like a volcano erupting."

Where did Ginger turn?

"I learned I could depend only on the Lord," she says.

"I kept myself and the children in the church even though it was so small I was the only divorced person in it. They certainly did not know what to do with me, but I knew God wanted me in that church."

Karen, on the other hand, did not have a Christian background or faith. "After our divorce I tried to cope by the usual route taken by my friends," she reflected. "I began bar-hopping, searching for a relationship that would dull the pain."

Then Karen's husband asked if they could try again, so they were remarried. This time the marriage lasted a year. (I've learned, incidentally, that speedy reconciliations too often lead to speedy separations.) This time God intervened in Karen's life to provide a different kind of stabilizer.

"One day at work a fellow worker shared a lot about Jesus Christ with me," she continued, "and I accepted His offer of forgiveness and a new life. Unbelievably, that very night my husband left! Oh, how much that hurt, but I now had a new source of strength and friendship. Now I did not need the bar scene, for I had Jesus Christ to turn to."

For some women, children become the stabilizer.

"For many years after our divorce my children were my therapy. I hid behind them because I was scared to date, afraid of rejection," confessed Ann.

Nancy had a daughter only five years old when she experienced divorce. "The best times for me after my divorce were when my daughter and I prayed together," she recalled. "Many times the Lord spoke to me through the simple prayers of my child. This helped me attach my anchor tightly to the Lord, and He gave me strength to go through things I didn't think I could ever make it through."

THE SEARCH FOR A STABILIZER

Most divorced singles have great difficulty finding a stabilizer. Many of them first try to stabilize their life after divorce by jumping into another relationship. This is particularly true if they seek help from other divorced non-Christian friends, who may "help" them enter the bar and bed scene.

The first thing I tell newly-divorced women is this: "*Stay away* from well-meaning friends, relatives, dating services, and matrimonial services—all who want to set you up with dates. Dating too soon actually destabilizes your life."

It's my experience that the recovery time after a divorce normally takes much longer than most people realize—often as long as five years. Dating too quickly and developing a new intimate relationship may actually hamper or stall the recovery process.

Another factor to consider is that dating too soon after divorce may retard the recovery of your child. "I started dating a guy weeks after the divorce," Jill told me. "I thought he could do no wrong. We got into a lot of things for which I am now sorry. My son was old enough to see what I was into with the guy I was dating. Our family life was in upheaval, with my ex-husband throwing it up against me with my son. Eventually I saw how wrong it was, that as long as this new man was in my life I wasn't really there for my son."

Remember Susan in chapter 1, the woman who endured her husband's affairs? She reports, "I was so devastated by my husband demeaning how I looked that I responded quickly to any man who paid attention to me. I was looking for a boost to my ego and got it from the first man who dated me. But I certainly did not find stability in relationships, because I went through seventeen relationships in a year and a half. I finally stopped dating abruptly when a man I was dating, a close friend of the family, sexually molested my daughter."

Another activity that looks like such a good stabilizer is an intensive Bible study. After all, shouldn't you learn more about God? Turning to God is important, but if you remember the energy illustration from the previous chapter, you may have only 5 percent of your mental energy at your disposal. That's not enough to do an intensive Bible study that requires you to concentrate for long periods of time on homework.

In addition, sitting in a Bible study group with emotionally secure women who appear to have it all together is a terrifying experience when you are falling apart emotionally, physically, spiritually, and even mentally. What you don't need is an unattainable role model—at least not for the first few months right after the divorce. Later on you will need this kind of intensive Bible study, but not right away.

Alcohol or drugs of any kind may also appear to provide a stabilizer that will give you the strength to cope with the tough months and years after divorce. However, use of chemicals to ease the pain can lead to addictions that will only drag you down further and could destroy your children. What you need is genuine support that can help you achieve stability.

Spiritual Support

Through the more than twenty years I have been working with divorced people I have discovered it consistently true that *the most effective support system for divorced singles is the church.*

Even though you may feel uncomfortable at first,

you and the children must both find a receptive church if you want to gain support quickly. Listen to Susan's experience:

"I kept on teaching Bible classes even during our separation. When my kids and I moved to another state I immediately connected with the church. We went Sunday morning and evening and Wednesday night as well. Though they had no singles group, they enfolded us with love and acceptance.

"Then I went back to my husband and we were remarried for nine months, only to break up again. The church I had started attending before rejoining my husband sent a couple to bring me back. The pastor, who had grown children, became a surrogate dad for my two girls. What a blessing that was!"

Not every church provides that kind of supportive environment. However, the simple fact of your commitment to stay with the church will provide spiritual stability for you. And staying with the church reduces the amount of change you are experiencing, and the stress of more upheaval. Remember the change curve? Limit all the changes you can.

Emotional Support
Another step that can help you transition into becoming an effective single parent is to *get into a group of people of similar age who are facing the same struggles.* You can find great comfort and encouragement in seeing that others know how you feel—and may even be in worse circumstances than you are. You also will meet those who are further along in their recovery and can offer you invaluable insight and encouragement.

For example, you might be really angry about having to move into a smaller house or apartment . . . until you discover another single parent who lives in a rat-infested apartment. You may be angry about your ex-husband's failure to pay child-support . . . until another woman walks in with black eyes and a broken arm from being beaten up by an ex who broke down the front door.

You'll be able to handle your experiences a lot better than the feelings you'd have in a well-ordered, middle-income couples Bible study group, where you are reminded of just how much you've lost. But take whatever emotional support you can get wherever you can find it, because later you will be able to give it to others: "Praise be to the God and Father of our Lord Jesus Christ, the Father of compassion and the God of all comfort, who comforts us in all our troubles, so that we can comfort those in any trouble with the comfort we ourselves have received from God" (2 Corinthians 1:3-4, NIV). Remember that our God is a God of hope and comfort.

"For three years I was a walking dead person," confesses Ginger. "I was really bad off emotionally. I'd get through the day at the office and fall apart at night when I got home."

Ginger heard that the singles group at our church in Modesto was huge. But with so little energy left for anything but work and sleep, she made no contact. Then she discovered some of her friends at work were part of the group. Eventually she joined and found help immediately.

"I heard about reconciliation and struggled with that. But I also saw my sons stabilize as they got into their own groups," Ginger recounted.

Though Kathy had been a church secretary when her husband found another woman and left her, she walked away from the church after divorce. Yet the Lord did not leave her alone. A friend gave her a copy of my book, *Too Close, Too Soon*, and she found it helpful.

"Eventually I picked up a Bible and began reading it," Kathy said. "Then I got information on a singles conference and walked into the church to see how it felt. I stayed and really found help."

Loving Support

This may surprise you, but another great support system for most divorced singles is their family. I tell our singles to grab the church with one hand and their family with the other. That's the quickest way to gain stability because it keeps both hands occupied.

"For the first year after my divorce my two daughters and I lived with my parents," Susan remembered. "They were not well off, having suffered some heavy financial reverses because of health problems, but they shared what they had. My mother helped me get my first job since high school in the customer service department of a department store. Then when my sister moved to California, she took us with her, pulling our belongings in a trailer."

You may even find that your ex in-laws are a surprisingly strong support immediately after your divorce. They are often distressed at their son's actions and will encourage you. Accept all the support they can give, for in about a year the pendulum probably will swing back to their son, who will be reconciled with his parents, brothers, and sisters. Remember that blood is thicker than water.

Susan certainly found that true. "Initially my ex-husband's parents were really upset with him. His father was an extremely conservative and strict pastor, so he was horrified when he learned about the sexual promiscuity of his son. As a result I received solid support and my daughters received gifts at Christmas and their birthdays, but that soon tapered off. Today my ex-husband's parents pay hardly any attention to their grandchildren."

Financial Support
Finding adequate assistance on financial matters is often the most difficult dilemma, since husbands often control the home's finances. You may not be aware of many of the expenses connected with your home. But you must determine the financial level at which you can function.

More important than anything else is to get onto a cash basis. If you have credit card bills, pay them off as soon as possible and then cancel the accounts, or at least lock the cards away. Set up a budget that you can live with over the long haul.

Next comes the hard part—for all of us. *You must limit yourself strictly to what you can afford, no matter how little it is.* The plain truth is that most single parents have to establish a financial plan that does not even take child-support into consideration, since the 1990 Census Bureau Survey data shows only 44 percent received full child-support, and 56 percent some or no support.

As part of your financial planning you'll want to learn exactly what resources you still have under your control. Are there items around your home—don't forget to look in the basement, garage, and closets—that could be sold? Then you will need to evaluate what you can do without and sell. As heartbreaking as it may be, you may need to consider even selling the house, as well as other valuables, including an expensive car. The proceeds from a garage sale can provide extra cash as well. I know this will be painful. However, because most divorces bring financial hardships to women, it must be done in almost all cases.

One caution: *Don't make rash decisions about material things that you will regret later, but do try your best to adjust your lifestyle to match your reduced income*. Perhaps a friend or family member who has experienced divorce can offer you advice as you make decisions on what to sell. Try to get some sound advice from trustworthy individuals who have all 25 percent of their mental energy.

A STABILIZATION PLAN

Most single parents assume that if you do the right things the pain of divorce and single parenting will simply go away. The corollary assumption is that if the pain does *not* go away, then you're doing something wrong.

I'm here to tell you that becoming a single parent and going through the recovery process is *always* painful. Even doing the right things will leave you with extreme pain—but doing the wrong things will result in excruciating pain. My goal in this book is to help you *minimize* the pain—don't try to get rid of it by taking attempted shortcuts to recovery. Healing is a painful experience. There's just no getting around it.

I recommend a four-part recovery process called SELF to describe the process of support and then the stabilization after a divorce. This process can be compared to the free fall you experience when you slip on a mountain slope, begin to slide, and then can't seem to find anything to grab hold of as you go sliding down the slope. The most vital thing in a divorce trauma is *to somehow come to a stop*—to find support in whatever way you can.

Next you need to get your bearings, stand up, and start moving away from the cliff. That is *stabilization*. The full process of finding support and becoming stabilized often takes as long as five years.

This acrostic, SELF, will help you remember the steps in the support and stabilization process:

Stabilize Yourself:
Spiritually
Emotionally
Lovingly
Financially

Stabilize Yourself Spiritually

Spiritual stabilization involves making sure you're drawing on the resources that only God can provide after your divorce. The issues here start with the basics: *Is Jesus Christ standing at the center of your life? Is He truly the Lord of your life?* The following simple steps will enable you to make Him the Lord of your life:

1. If He never has been Lord of your life:

- Admit to God that you are a sinner (Romans 3:23).
- Confess that Jesus Christ is God in the flesh.
- Pray this prayer word for word with a sincere heart: "Lord Jesus, I admit that I am separated from You and I ask that You forgive my sins and make me into the person You want me to be."
- Find a Bible-believing church this week and join it.
- Start reading the Gospel of John in the New Testament.

2. If He has been Lord of your life in the past:

- Admit to God that you have drifted away.
- Confess that Jesus Christ is God in the flesh.
- Pray this prayer: "Lord Jesus, I admit that I am separated from You and I ask that You forgive my sins and make me into the person You want me to be."
- Find a Bible-believing church this week and join it.

- Start reading the Gospel of John in the New Testament.

3. If He is Lord of your life:

- Thank Him for what He has done in your life.
- Reconfirm that Jesus Christ is God come in the flesh.
- Pray this prayer: "Lord Jesus, thank You for what You have done for me and use me to comfort others with Your comfort."
- Find a ministry in the church you belong to.
- Start reading the book of Romans.

You may be terribly busy and stressed out, but force yourself to have a consistent time of spending even a few minutes reading several verses in the Bible daily (the Psalms are a great place to start), letting God speak to you through His Word.

Your relationship needs *are* great, but your need for strong Christian fellowship is even greater. You need to be with people who can help you establish or maintain a spiritual growth pattern in your life. Doing so will help give you resources of strength that you can share with your children and others.

So where can you find this fellowship? You may not attend a church large enough to have a singles group. If it doesn't, don't withdraw from your church just because the people there don't seem to understand you or provide an adequate supportive environment. Reach out to other singles in the church on your own. Be creative and look for opportunities to serve.

Here's an idea: If you're in a church that has at least a few single parents, you may want to do what one of the single parents I know does in her church. She uses some of her free time to visit other single parents, and by using a survey form she finds out what needs they may have for food, clothing, and other household goods. Then she reports these needs to the benevolence committee of her church. Financial help then flows back to those families. The happiness this brings is my friend's biggest reward.

Stabilize Yourself Emotionally

Remember that after your divorce you may be expending 85 percent or more of your energy trying to control emotional reactions. You will experience violent ups and downs as you struggle with why you and your husband could not make it together. Often you will be extremely angry at your ex-husband, many times for very good reasons. One lady says her favorite book is one on how to load and fire a .38-caliber revolver.

Consider Kathy's experience. Although the marriage had not been a very good one, even so when her husband found another woman and asked for a divorce, Kathy experienced enormous emotional pain. Kathy then started to date. Driving to work one day, her car engine suddenly stopped. She called a friend who was a mechanic. He discovered that not only had her ex put a destructive chemical in her gasoline, he had loosened the brakes. Really angry now, she documented what had happened with legal authorities.

Then Kathy's husband stopped paying child support and alimony. Kathy hauled him into court for contempt, asking that his wages be attached. He was furious. Working with the district attorney she reached an agreement that he would stop harassing her and damaging her property in return for her not attaching his wages. (Remember the steps of destruction in chapter 2?)

Yet the amount of emotional energy consumed during experiences like this is enormous. It will leave you worn out and exhausted. Only as your spiritual health improves and strengthens over time will you find yourself able to set up boundaries to contain these emotional gyrations.

As you learn to walk in obedience, and trust the power of the Holy Spirit, you will find yourself getting an emotional lift. Experiencing the reality of God's love and forgiveness and learning to trust Him becomes a powerful emotional stabilizer. Making a list of positives in your life will give you emotional balance and a list of praises to give back to God.

Stabilizing Yourself Lovingly

A third step in regaining stability is to carefully reestablish your "loving support system." I find that when families get into crisis, most of them begin to cut themselves off from the extended family. Both sets of in-laws are isolated, including aunts and uncles. The members of the "family in trouble" do not attend family reunions, preferring to pull back into a corner and fight it out among themselves.

Once the family breaks apart, you must rebuild your loving support system, going back to not only your parents but also your aunts and uncles for the sake of you and your kids. If, for example, it becomes apparent that your ex-husband was the problem, you may get some strong support from your parents-in-law, depending on what your relationship with them has been like. As I said earlier, however, your positive relationship with them may be short-lived.

To help you reestablish your loving support system, instead of taking a vacation just with the kids, consider a visit to your parents, your brothers and sisters, or other relatives. Typically they will be quite supportive and concerned for you and the children. But they will also be sympathetic and provide support on other levels, such as Susan's mother finding a job for Susan.

Look up aunts and uncles you haven't seen in years. Rebuild those family contacts. You will find that the further out you get in the circle of family relationships, the less concerned they will be about the details of your divorce. Most likely they'll just be happy someone is trying to reestablish the family ties and eager to stand by you in your time of need.

I've seen some single moms get a lot of satisfaction out of working on a family genealogy. They use that as a project to help them get the focus off themselves and develop a big picture of how broad their support system really is.

Stabilizing Yourself Financially

Gaining financial stability is vital to maintaining long-term emotional stability. However, if you focus on the financial aspect first and force the issue, you may not have the emotional and spiritual support for the long haul, and therefore you might make some tragic financial mistakes. Once you're making progress spiritually and emotionally, you will be able to tackle the financial issues more effectively.

As I said earlier, it's important to get off credit and onto a cash basis as quickly as possible. Balance your budget. Sell all the assets you can to reduce your debt load. Remember, the Census Bureau report indicates that family income drops 37 percent within four months of separation.

Few single parents realize it quickly enough, but because less income is usually available, you probably will need to reduce your standard of living significantly.

For example, if your annual family income before divorce was $30,000, you may hope you only have to slip back to $25,000. Unfortunately, for most people $18,000 is a much more realistic figure. If your family income was $60,000, plan on getting along on about $37,000, or even less if you do not have exceptionally good job skills.

Although I hope you're one of the rare ones, prepare yourself to live without child-support. In the United States less than 25 percent of all child-support is ever fully paid. Single parents who refuse to come to grips with this fact often end up with huge financial problems, perhaps even bankruptcy. Unfortunately, that is an all too frequent scenario, since *75 percent of all single parents experience bankruptcy at one time or another, and 60 percent of single-parent children live in rentals and are classified as poor* by the Census Bureau Surveys.

If you own a house, your biggest financial decision will probably be whether or not to sell it. The tendency is to hang on as long as you can until your situation is desperate. But then you may have to sell at too low a price, and you'll lose your equity — *and* the ability to buy another home. So if finances are a problem I usually recommend selling the house at the best possible moment. Seek wise counsel from several people who are knowledgeable and deeply committed to *your* best interests.

I know of a situation in which the wife is determined to stay in the house — and the husband is determined to punish her by not making house payments. In six weeks or more the house will go into foreclosure and the mortgage company will get around $35,000 in equity because she won't sell and he won't pay.

Ginger was more realistic. Even though she and her husband had shared a lovely home, after their divorce she let the house be sold and the proceeds divided. With her portion she was able to make a down payment on a small house. Then she set up one room as a business, using her skill as a hairdresser. Even though there was "never enough" money, she was able to keep this house, especially since her ex consistently paid his child-support.

After the divorce you may need to find a job. That's never easy, but it is possible, even though in some cases the day-care expense may be high—perhaps more than the job pays. I know a single parent who worked eight-hour days in a fast-food restaurant. At $3.50 an hour she got $25 per day after taxes and paid $15 for child-care. That left her with only $10 per day remaining.

Yet you have to start somewhere or you never get to work your way up. The Census Survey reports that single parents tend to be less educated, more unemployed, and in lower income brackets than standard families. That just means you have to work harder.

Ann is a classic example of a single parent who worked her way up. After her divorce she went on Aid for Families with Dependent Children (AFDC) while she went back to school. She then worked in a hospital kitchen. She quickly determined that she did not want to do that all her life, so she took the training to wire personal computer boards. After working in that field, she switched to a bank, where for eight years she worked with lost and stolen credit cards.

By this time her children had married and divorced, so Ann adopted two of her grandchildren, one of whom had cerebral palsy. The state asked her to stay home and care for this child, which she did for the next ten years. Then she got permission to go back to work, since almost all of the symptoms of cerebral palsy had disappeared. Ann is currently working in the district attorney's office with victims of child abuse.

Nancy had a large, gorgeous home but lost everything during the separation and divorce; she received no spousal support or child-support. But she got a job with a bonus system, where she could earn extra money. I helped her set goals for herself and her daughter, and exactly five years after her divorce she moved into her own home.

In most cases I recommend that the newly-divorced not go back to school for the first year after the divorce. What I have seen happen all too often is that single parents simply don't have the mental and physical energy to do well in the classroom initially.

Remember the 5 percent mental and 5 percent physical circles? (See figure 3 on pages 28-29.) Picture a woman who enrolls and starts classes with great enthusiasm. Then when she is assigned several books to read and five papers to write, discouragement sets in. Often she quits school — and now has another "failure" to deal with. If she waits, in about a year she will be far enough along in her recovery process to do the assignments and stay on top of the classwork.

SUMMARY

Remember these principles for the stabilizing process:

Avoid the quick fix of another relationship.

Take the time to recover fully; don't settle for just any man.

Really stabilize your SELF.

Finding stabilizers in your new life as a single parent is vital. But just as vital is resetting your expectations. We'll work on that in the next chapter.

FOUR

Resetting Expectations

L ife has a way of playing what appears to be a cruel hoax on the single parent.

When you finally get the divorce, you feel the transition to a normal new life is finally underway—and "normal life" should arrive any day. The pain and frustration you have experienced for so long is simply a blip on the screen—surely it's about to disappear.

Some new single moms still secretly hope that their ex-husband will "come around" and recognize the error of his ways. Maybe God will even zap him in some way to straighten him out. And he'll probably be back before long.

Certainly the children can be depended on for love and stability, to get the family back to normal behavior. After all, they chose to live with you over their dad. Sure, he has visitation rights, but if you treat your kids right, they'll probably never want to live with him.

Oh sure, you still feel on the verge of tears most of the time, and you do find yourself walking around like a zombie more often than you'd like to admit. But this too will pass. It won't be long and you'll be on top of things, if you can just hang on. Right?

"NORMAL" IS AN EMPTY DREAM

Wrong! The reality is that the "normal" you may be longing for is an empty dream. And as long as you hang on to it, you're in effect *backing into the future,* dragging your kids with you. You will continually trip over the past instead of realistically coming to terms with the future.

Unless you face the reality of your new situation as a single parent, you will keep resetting your internal clock of expectations for the future—*when* you get married, *when* all the bills are paid, *when* the kids are all in school, *when* you lose weight . . . on and on. Every time you reset your clock on the hopes of the future, you sink deeper into depression instead of catching up or getting ahead of the changes that are happening to you. This can be an endless treadmill that uses all your energy but gets you nowhere.

If you don't leave the past behind, you may embark on a number of changes just to tread water. For example, you may enter a new relationship to deaden the pain of breakup and to help restore your self-esteem. Or you may visit other churches to see if you can put the events of the past on hold. But every step into the past only leaves you feeling more empty because *you're avoiding reality.*

YESTERDAY IS GONE

The fact is that the chances of your husband coming back next week penitently and ready to start over are almost nonexistent in the first few months. The Census Survey states that 70 percent of divorces end in marriage. Your ex may have started a relationship before he left you and therefore is already planning a new marriage. In time he may cycle back to you for reconciliation, but you have to take this time to stabilize yourself.

Your children may be truly supportive of you now, but you can almost count on it—one day your son will want to live with his dad and you'll feel betrayed. Although your kids are behaving well now, later they may go through a period of extreme rebelliousness because they haven't dealt with their own feelings of guilt and abandonment.

Most significantly, you probably will need about five years of healing before feeling you have truly recovered from the trauma of the divorce. If you have just experienced divorce that may seem pretty incredible, but I assure you this span of time has proven reliable with hundreds of women I know. Listen to what Jill told me: "When you whipped out the information that it would take five years to recover I said to myself, 'He's nuts.' Looking back now I can confirm that I started feeling like a human being again after five years."

A confirmation also comes from Kathy: "I truly believe in the five-year theory. Looking back, I was finally coming together by then." For the reality of hope to take hold, it requires time to allow God to work in your life.

PATHWAYS TO RECOVERY

Getting rid of false expectations is one of the first steps to recovery. But setting realistic expectations for the future does not come easily. Let's look at some pathways to recovery that focus on expectations.

Acknowledging Anger
One good sign I look for is when the single mom is finally able to feel anger. Most recovering single parents need to

experience a heavy dose of revenge to snap out of the preoccupation with the past.

This may happen after an ex-husband has not paid the child-support for a month. Or maybe he brought his girlfriend along when he came in his new car to pick up the children for the weekend. Or "she" comes to the door to get his kids and gives you the child-support check "she" has written on their joint bank account. For many single moms, when "she" gets involved in the flow of money and visitation it's like they've grabbed hold of a wire with 44,000 volts.

At this point most single moms feel a surge of raw rage. They can cheerfully imagine putting their hands over their ex's ears and squeezing his head until something pops. Or clawing his eyes out. Anything to release the anger.

Such anger is actually healthy because *it's an indicator of progress* — it shows you're beginning to heal. If you don't control it, however, the anger can get out of hand. I once had a man call me and say, "Jim, you've gotta help me. My wife's just gone crazy." We drove to his house and there she was, throwing all of his stuff onto the front lawn in a driving rain: guns, clothes, electronic equipment, everything.

Once that rage expresses itself in any way, the single mom may realize, "I'm kind of a dangerous woman now. I have to learn how to control my emotions." When that happens I often suggest she read *The Christian Use of Emotional Power,* by Norman Wright.[1] She needs to learn how to channel her new feelings constructively rather than destructively.

At this time I also show her the progress she's beginning to make by introducing her to a recovery checklist (see figure 4) from my book *Reconcilable Differences.*[2]

Figure 4
Recovery Checklist

❏ 1. *Finances:* Are you able to stand on your own and meet your own needs? This may mean being willing to drop several levels on the socioeconomic ladder and live on less.

❏ 2. *Schedule:* Are you getting up on time, getting enough sleep, taking care of yourself, and keeping appointments?

❏ 3. *Legal:* Are you willing to stop the divorce process and allow reconciliation a chance? This means showing a stance of openness.

❏ 4. *Rational:* Are you willing to put aside your anger and bitterness and act like a mature adult? You can't blame the "friend" for everything, because it takes two people.

❏ 5. *Spiritual:* Are you a member actively involved in a local church? When your life is unstable, you need the strength and support of other believers.

❏ 6. *In-Laws:* Are you willing to be civil and friendly toward your in-laws? You need all the support you and your children can get. They are still your children's grandparents. Remember, friendliness begets friendliness.

❏ 7. *Commitment:* Are you stable enough to make a sincere commitment to reconciliation for one year? Many think it's easier to get married, but how stable can that commitment be?

❏ 8. *Counsel:* Are you seeking counsel from those over you, according to Hebrews 13:17? This is a time for objective, biblical directives to prevent you from cycling back to a second marriage and possibly a second divorce.

❏ 9. *Guidance:* Are you willing to put in the time, effort, and energy to demonstrate that you are open to instruction? The test here is to see if you are willing to learn from your mistakes.

❑ 10. *Singleness:* Can you be single and content? It is important that you be able to stand by yourself emotionally before you move on to reconcile or meet someone else.

❑ 11. *Friendships:* Are you able to have a healthy same-sex friendship? Lack of close friends will force you to expect too much of anyone in a relationship.

❑ 12. *Devotions:* Are you consistent in your time with the Lord in prayer and study of the Word? This time provides all the vitamins for your spiritual and emotional development.

❑ 13. *Grace:* Are you open to God's directions to His prophet Hosea? In order to understand God's grace toward us, we need to extend it to others.

❑ 14. *Emotional:* Are you able to control your emotions for short periods of time? The first step is to go one day at a time and then build stability on that.

❑ 15. *Guilt:* Are you willing to ask forgiveness for the wrongs you committed in the marriage? If we expect others to do something, we have to lead by example.

It's also helpful for her to record items such as the first day she can go four hours without crying about the divorce, then eight hours without crying, then a whole day without crying, and eventually a week, a month, and a year. Those are major milestones that need to be recognized and recorded for personal encouragement.

Resetting Economic Expectations

The sooner economic expectations are reset the better. Many new single moms seem to think that life can go on as usual with the perks that make them feel good—frequent hair appointments, having her nails done, or even a new wardrobe.

One time a single mom with two children was in a real financial bind. In order to correct the situation it seemed to me she needed to consider two things, one major and the other not so catastrophic but important. First, she needed to consider selling her house; second, she needed to stop getting her nails done weekly. Tears flowed down her cheeks as she said "Jim, I can't do that. All that's left of my self-esteem is my nails."

But she made the tough choice on the nails. Three months later she came back and said, "I have some extra money now, but I've had to learn to live without having my nails done."

About six months later she came to me again and showed me her hands: "Look at my nails! I've got a good job, and I'm stabilized. I can do this now. And it's good for me. But I understand that I was using bread money to have my nails done, and that was not good. My folks helped me keep up the house payments until I got settled on my job. Thank you for the hard advice!"

This principle bears repeating: *in almost every case, a newly-divorced woman cannot maintain her level of pre-divorce lifestyle by herself.* In fact, dropping down two economic levels is likely. Why two? The Census Survey states that 50 percent of single moms don't work, and 40 percent of single moms who don't remarry end up on AFDC.

If you drop down one level and still can't make ends meet, then dropping the second time is really devastating. If you go down two levels and stabilize your budget, it's a whole lot more fun to start going up one level. But if you try to maintain a lifestyle that protects your self-esteem at the expense of providing adequate food, clothes, and some extras for your children, your guilt will overwhelm any advantage to your self-esteem.

Remember that on average, because expenses climb dramatically when the family unit breaks apart (two residences, attorney fees, etc.), total family income drops 37 percent in the first four months of separation, according to the Census Survey.

Building Healthy Self-Esteem

Please don't get the impression that I'm downgrading the value of self-esteem. But instead of trying to build self-esteem from possessions and disappointing relationships, you need healthy contacts with other people—and that's where I see the church fitting in.

Single parents can move up a notch in their self-esteem while they're under the umbrella of the church, unless they happen to be in one where the counselor or pastor will take advantage of them sexually. (Sadly, this is a growing area of concern for emotionally vulnerable people.)

Healthy self-esteem must begin on the spiritual level. Only when single parents become spiritually stabilized—knowing they have a Savior who unconditionally accepts them—are they in a position to feel good about themselves emotionally.

You simply can't have a sound basis for self-esteem in looking nice and appearing successful. But that is where many single moms are because in today's society self-esteem is often tied to what you *have*. This attitude is developed early in life. In junior high, for example, status is based not on how much your father makes but on whether you have a boyfriend. If you don't have a boyfriend you feel like a social outcast. No wonder that as an adult a woman has the expectation that she will get her self-esteem back when she has another mate. This feeds the drive to remarry.

Many people who divorce appear to have been emotionally "one-legged" people. They used marriage as their leg of self-esteem, but when that was yanked out from under them they began to wobble and eventually fell because they had only one leg left to stand on.

This is why everyone needs to learn to get self-worth from a relationship with God through Jesus Christ and the church family.

Financial Planning

One single mom I know, who has four children, was really struggling. I helped her learn a basic approach to financial planning that works—even when there is little income and few resources. Very simply, we decided what had to be paid first when she got some money, especially when she received her paycheck. The money left was placed in envelopes labeled utilities, insurance, food, etc., and sealed. The appropriate envelope was only to be opened when it was time to pay that particular bill.

This single mom understood the procedure, but one day she came to me and said excitedly, "I've sent off for a complete Bible study program!" It was too late by that time to stop the order, so she received three boxes—one with a bookcase, another with tapes, and a third with study materials for a whole year.

The cost? Every month she was to pay thirty-five dollars—thirty-five dollars desperately needed to pay her utility bills. There was no way she could handle an additional monthly payment on top of it.

I had to say to her, "I know you're eager to study the Bible, but you must return these materials. You can't do this at the expense of food, lights, and gas."

Resetting the Kids' Expectations

Children in a single-parent home also have to reset their expectations. For the first three months after the divorce, Mom is often so wounded emotionally that she has a hard time functioning at all. Some women may not even be able to get out of bed all day. One of the children, even a child as young as nine, may have to quickly take on the role of a parent. You'll find this nine-year-old fixing the dinner, cleaning the house, doing the wash. It may take six months or more for the family to redistribute the workload.

If Mom had not been working outside the home, when she gets a job, suddenly she has little energy and time to spend on simple things like doing the laundry, cooking dinner, or cleaning the house. And again the children will have to pitch in.

After the initial emotional stresses ease, the single-parent mom often begins filling in on the activities a father usually does. Where I live, these moms haul their kids to soccer, baseball, and football games. Interestingly, the only time some of these single moms ever see their ex-husbands is at the game when the men come to see their children play. And that is where a lot of reconciling begins to take place as the two root for their kids, sharing that common experience. But only if he leaves his girlfriend at home.

After the first year, single moms can gain valuable parenting information and reset their expectations regarding their children by getting involved in a mixed group of married and single parents. As an example, a single mom needs to see a married couple with teenagers who have the same kinds of problems as her own teens. She'll see a father and mother bicker with each other in a Bible study. That's a real encouragement, for she says to herself,

"I may have the same problems with my teen that they do, but at least I don't have to fight with my mate about it."

Resetting Expectations About Remarriage

I'm convinced that in today's complex social environment single moms ought to reset their expectations regarding another marriage. Blending together a new family unit is a delicate process. In addition, there are new dangers created by the sexual attitudes and behaviors of single or divorced men.

Now I know that what I have to say may not be great news. One reason is that your father may have contributed significantly to your sense of significance and self-worth. When you were married, your husband—at least initially—functioned in the same way. So it's only natural that you want to look for another long-term relationship that will provide the same security and sense of self-esteem. You also naturally would like to find a permanent father for your children, especially if they're boys.

Unfortunately, the social scene, even in today's churches, has changed so dramatically over the past five to ten years that I now urge the single mom to readjust expectations regarding remarriage, and to consider not remarrying until after the children are grown. "Are you crazy?" you ask. Before you slam this book shut, at least let me explain my thinking.

One of the sobering new realities is the explosion of sexually transmitted diseases. In my two decades of ministry I have interviewed over ten thousand singles, most of them divorced and sexually active. Because the majority of singles, even in the church, are sexually active, the danger of contracting sexually transmitted diseases, including AIDS, is climbing steadily.

Because of its long incubation period (five to fifteen

years), AIDS in particular is not easily detectable, revealing no symptoms during that incubation period. Yet anyone with the HIV virus will pass it on during sexual activity. And condoms do not provide full protection since they have at least a 10 percent failure rate, and according to the U.S. Center for Disease Control the virus has been shown to pass through most condoms.[3] I'd prefer to see a single mom who is struggling to raise her children avoid that danger. When you have sex with someone, you are having sexual contact with everyone he has had sex with for the past fifteen years.

The story of Susan, told earlier, illustrates another extremely dangerous element in dating and remarrying. The man she dated was an upstanding member in both her church and the medical community, yet later he sexually molested her nine-year-old daughter. Of the single moms in our church group, one-third insist that their ex-husbands sexually molested their children. These men are now circulating—looking for other relationships with women, many of whom have children.

Another issue in hasty remarriage is the risk of marrying someone you know very little about. Once upon a time we all lived in small communities where John had to pass muster with Dad before he could date Jane. Once he was dating Jane, he had to pass muster with her grandfather, her uncles Abe and Ralph, and close friends. There was little these folk did not know about John, for they were there when he got drunk or lost his cool and flared up angrily in a ballgame. The family knew how many girls he had already jilted, and whether he had fathered any illegitimate children.

Most single moms are not able to discover this kind of information in today's highly mobile and impersonal society. The most pleasing conversationalist and most fun-loving date may be the biggest rascal, but you may never know it until you get married.

SUMMARY

Resetting expectations is tough, and often happens only after tough negative experiences. And unless a single parent is in a good divorce recovery group in a church, she will possibly never think through the kinds of issues raised in this chapter.

Keep these principles in mind for resetting your expectations:

Reset your recovery time — think in terms of five years.

Take the time to recover before you go on to another relationship.

Quarantine yourself from AIDS by living a celibate life.

In the next chapter we'll take a look at parenting issues and attempt to come to terms with your children's special needs.

FIVE

Recognizing the Special Needs of Your Children

"**M**om, look at this fish I caught today! Isn't it a big one?" Billy exclaimed as he left the van and ran up the sidewalk to meet his mother, Ellen. "I caught it all by myself. They said I could bring it home with me."

Billy proudly showed off his three-quarter-pound trout as his mother admired it.

"That's a lovely fish, Billy. I can tell you're proud of it," she said enthusiastically. "Did the other boys catch one as well?"

"Yes, Mom, but mine is the biggest," he exclaimed. "Some of the kids threw theirs back because they were too small."

Ellen could see what a proud moment this was in the life of her son, who rarely saw his father and had never gone fishing with him. She decided to capture the moment as a reminder to both Billy and herself of the joy good times with others can bring us. With money from her parents she had a taxidermist mount the catch with the same care reserved for a trophy fish.

NEEDED: MALE ROLE MODEL

Billy is representative of all the boys who miss their dad at an age when they need his role model the most. And his mom was far enough in her personal recovery from divorce to recognize the special needs of her son. She accepted the opportunity to send her son with several men at the church when they volunteered to go fishing with a group of boys being raised in single-parent homes.

Billy's experience reminds me of my own after my father left. Some of my friends in the church and their dads took me fishing. I also went hunting with other friends and their fathers. In this way many of my needs were met through the secondary relationships found in my peer group.

Terri Speicher, a single mom who is raising four sons, has written, "I have experienced God's promise to provide fathering in expected and unexpected places." The first place she discovered that extra dimension of fathering was in her family—the uncles and grandfathers.

"We've gone out of our way to spend time with our scattered grandfathers and uncles. We either invite their families to visit, or we make the long trips to their homes on the East and West Coasts.

"The men in the family are 'available.' Uncle Dick takes on all youthful challengers to his title as 'Scrabble King' during our annual Thanksgiving reunion. One Uncle Bob rules the basketball court; the other Uncle Bob takes my boys individually on ski vacations. (My son) Paul gets loving guidance and encouragement during his dad's visits and frequent telephone conversations. . . . Yet distance prevents our families from the consistent hands-on fathering my boys need. The Lord revealed other sources to me."

Terri found that Sunday school teachers and Christian camp counselors also can meet special needs. Friends from the church have taken the boys to ballgames and have even dropped by for Ping-Pong or backyard basketball.[1]

Good male role models may take some effort to locate, but the results are well worth it.

DO GIRLS COPE BETTER?

Single moms tend to have an easier time with daughters than with sons. That's not only because they're the same sex, but because girls tend to have more channels for coping with the pain of divorce than do boys. For example, some girls will imagine their whole family is still together and fantasize a whole range of family experiences. In general, girls also read a lot more than boys and are able to transfer their own experiences to those of the characters in the story.

STAGES OF AWARENESS

In many cases, the newly-divorced mom is hardly aware of the special needs of her children. I describe the first stage of post-divorce reaction to the kids' needs as *numbness*. The single mom is really caught up in her own grief and may be unavailable to the children for several weeks or even months. During this time a child may suddenly become the "adult" in the home and take on adult responsibilities.

Fifteen-year-old John, for example, took on his father's role when their home was broken into one night. He grabbed a baseball bat and drove off the intruder. For weeks he slept with his Little League baseball bat ready for immediate action.

Remember that these hurry-up growth experiences are not all bad. Some of them prepare boys for manhood.

The mom's second stage is *awareness*. As her emotional pain thaws she becomes aware that the children are in pain as well. Now she will begin to seek help for her kids, and the church can make a major contribution if it's truly aware of the need.

In many schools and churches today more than half of the children come from single-parent families. But too often this situation is not recognized and the special needs are not met.

I'm especially aware of and sensitive to the hunger for male attention that boys in single-parent families can have. Sometimes these boys come and just hang onto my leg because I am a man who knows them. In fact, in our church's single-parent family ministry, we regularly have boys going up to a man and saying, "Are you going to be my daddy?" They're looking for *anybody* who can fill the empty space in their life.

I must issue a strong word of caution at this point. Single moms who are aware of the intense needs of their sons may go to a third stage of response to the children which I call *over-reaction*. This is almost like a phobia. At this stage in their recovery single moms tend to exaggerate how bad their kids are doing. They'll spend one hundred dollars an hour for counseling for their kids or try to get them into awareness groups . . . anything to help them deal with the perceived pain.

Carol responded to her son Ivan's pain by illegally stopping all visitation with his father, and then forcing Ivan into counseling as well. Despite this, Ivan's problems intensified partly because of the loss of contact with his dad. In addition, finances forced Carol to stop the expensive counseling. Ivan remained cut off from his father and became very bitter. Often the cure can be worse than the illness.

No matter what the other parent has done, the contact must be maintained so that the child does not build a mental image of the other person that is not real. This includes cases in which abuse and molestation have occurred, which can be controlled by supervised visitation.

CAUTION: POTENTIAL DANGER AHEAD

Another set of problems can surface when single moms set out to put their boys into contact with a man to *replace* the father. You can imagine the emotions that surge when she sees her son open the door and ask her male friend, "Are you going to become my daddy?" She's so convinced of her son's need for a male model that she may marry a man too quickly just to relieve her anxiety.

At this stage of her recovery this is the worst possible motive for remarriage. Not only does it often push her into a loveless marriage, it also locks her into a marriage that will lose its reason for being when the children leave home. According to the district attorney in Modesto, where I live, 44 percent of all sexual child abuse cases being tried in our community involve a stepfather — so the risk of permanent damage to the child may be greater than the benefit. Even in a "standard family," 16 percent of molesters are the real fathers, 12 percent friends, 12 percent uncles, 12 percent grandfathers, 11 percent neighbors, and 12 percent stepmothers (molesting stepsons).

Vicki was struggling to recover from a violent divorce and also survive the terrible twos with her daughter, Whitney, when she met Vick. He was attractive and only just a "little bit" nonChristian. After a whirlwind courtship and marriage in Reno, all seemed well.

In just a few years, however, Whitney refused to be around Vick, and when she was seven finally told her mother about ongoing sexual abuse. Vicki is now twice divorced and bitter over the molestation. Giving at least one year to the courtship might have saved Whitney from this terrible experience.

Another danger is that the single mom may feel so desperate she will turn to almost any type of "big brother" program. She does not have the time to check out the men offering themselves as male models, and an organization also may not be doing a good job of screening its applicants. Also, the organization might not be able to legally discriminate against someone on a basis of sexual orientation. The worst-case scenario is that her boy may be sexually molested, and she may not become aware of it for many years—if ever.

I strongly recommend that you keep your children in the church and around Christian men. Unfortunately, even in church you still need to be careful and observant. Be especially suspicious if any man spends too much private time with your son.

Pay the price to get your boys to camp, even if it means skimping on something very important to you. They need environments where there is a lot of control and solid role modeling.

Don't change churches unless you have to. If you are going to move from one church to another, attempt to choose a church that's large enough that your children will encounter peers from school as well. That way the relationships they develop at church will continue during the week at school and prevent them from getting involved exclusively with nonChristian kids.

Be especially wary of the single man who, when he

comes for a date, seems to be more interested in spending time with your kids than with you. He'll approach you and be friendly with you, but his focused attention is on your child or children. Maybe his interest is authentic and wholesome, but maybe not. You may be tempted to relax your early warning system because you badly want your child's needs met. So be alert and look for those telltale signs of unhealthy interest in your child.

TREATING YOUR CHILD'S EMOTIONAL SHOCK

Although the single mom may overreact to the child's needs, it's equally important not to shortchange the child by under-estimating the emotional shock of suddenly living without a father. Most kids function adequately as they process the pain over a long period, but in some cases the emotions remain hidden, only to surface when children are in their twenties, or even older—as it did in my case.

I was already married when I suddenly found I needed to deal with strong internal pain. The pressure of getting married and working two jobs while going to college brought out some emotions that I had to deal with. As I learned more of what it meant to be a Christian husband, a flow of resentment against my father was released.

As the oldest child I had assumed the "father" role in the family at age twelve. My mother was working and attending college, so I felt really loaded down as I started junior high. In high school I felt I needed to work and give everything to the family. At the time I did not feel resentment, but after being married a few months the resentment overflowed.

I became so angry at my dad for leaving that one

day I walked up to a wall and drove my fist through it. This emotional and physical pain eventually forced me to forgive my dad and rebuild contact with him.

How does hidden pain surface and affect your child and those in her environment? How can you know that your child's coping mechanism is overloaded?

I find it shows up best in latent hostility or anger. Quick bursts of anger, excessive selfishness, dominating the mother's attention, and major behavioral changes are all possible indicators of a struggle with anger.

Regression is something else to be looking for. This is a pattern of turning to old habits, such as bedwetting. Children who are in regression may become just plain ornery and bad-mouth everything. Their report cards may reveal significantly lower grades. If they were faithful in cleaning their rooms, now they leave them a mess. They may stop brushing their teeth and try out very different hairstyles.

The alert mother is aware of these symptoms of regression and provides special attention and loving awareness, explaining that the behavior is not unexpected, and that she knows they will soon make progress again. More than anything, children need consistent discipline coupled with unconditional love.

But new single moms are often of little help to their children the first weeks—and sometimes months—after the divorce. In fact, the parent may initially be so dysfunctional that a nine- or ten-year-old can have more mental energy available for normal household activities.

This may seem strange, but I've had new single mothers call me up and ask, "Rev. Talley, should I fix dinner for my children tonight?"

This happens to people whose emotional trauma has robbed them of all decision-making ability. The energy needed to decide to fix a dinner and then identify what to prepare is simply not available at that stage.

When a call like this comes I may respond, "Why don't you ask your daughter?"

Rene is ten and nearby, so Mom asks, "Rene, should I fix dinner tonight?"

"Why sure, Mom, I'm hungry," she'll reply.

"What does Rene want for dinner?" I say.

"I want soup and hot dogs," Rene answers.

So I tell the mom that's what she ought to fix for dinner. And since Rene knew what she wanted, she'll be a lot of help to her mother.

This presence of mind in the child can be terribly deceiving, however, in the early weeks and months. Rene may appear to be perfectly normal and in control, but there is no doubt she's undergoing emotional upheaval, too. Though the trauma is not as obvious as her mother's, this internal stress will show up in a variety of ways.

Don't expect progress, advancement, and improvement in a number of areas of your child's development for at least a year. If, for example, Rene has been doing well at school, she probably will not accelerate that progress. In fact, it's more likely that her grades will go down and her relationships with other students deteriorate. Many new single parents expect their straight A student to keep on getting As after the divorce, and their whole world seems to come apart when the child brings home a B on the report card.

Let's consider a comparable situation. If your child had been ill for a year, missing most classes, would you expect her to be an A student when she finally recovers? Of course not, because it would take her quite a while to catch up. The same is true for the emotional distress of separation and divorce: Children need time to return to normal.

WHAT KIDS WOULD LIKE YOU TO KNOW

Myrle Carner, a detective for the Seattle Police Department, has dealt with hundreds of teenagers in crisis. These kids have parents like you and me. Carner writes, "I've talked to hundreds of parents who are upset, angry, and sad that their sons and daughters have wound up in trouble. These are not crazed, psychotic adults, but generally well-meaning moms and dads who live in your neighborhood, work hard, volunteer for the PTA, and then see the wholesome lives of their offspring unravel before their eyes."

Detective Carner has asked their teenaged sons and daughters this question: "If your parents were seated with us right now, what would you like to tell them?" Their answers can be summarized with these seven statements:

1. *Keep cool.* Don't lose your temper in a crunch. Don't blow your top when things go wrong. Kids need the reassurance that comes from controlled responses.

2. *Please show us who's boss.* Most young people want parents who are strict. Not a cruel parent beating them with a belt, but parents who are consistent and fair in discipline. Kids need the security of specific boundaries.

3. *Don't blow your class.* Translation: If you're forty, don't try to act sixteen. Kids want someone they can look up to. Be a parent, not a peer.

4. *Please, light a candle.* The kids Detective Carner talks to are saying, "Please tell us that God is not dead, sleeping, or on vacation. We need to believe in something bigger and stronger than ourselves."

5. *Scare the heck out of us.* Translation: Get tough, Mom. If you catch your kids lying, cheating, stealing, swearing, or boozing, then discipline them. Let them know that what they did was wrong. When they need punishment, dish it out. But also let them know you love

them, even when they let you down. Unconditional love coupled with consistent discipline really works.

6. *Call our bluff.* Did you know that kids don't really want all they ask for? They want parents who won't be intimidated when they threaten to drop out of school, or to run away from home. Do you think your child really wants to give up the comforts and security of home?

7. *Be honest with us.* It's no use trying to fool your kids. They know you better than you know yourself. They know when you're telling it like it is and when you're not. All kids want their folks to "be real."[2]

I consider children the most durable things God ever made, and am constantly amazed what they can live through. For more in-depth coverage on how to meet the emotional needs of your children, I recommend *How to Really Love Your Child* and the companion book *How to Really Love Your Teenager*, both by Dr. Ross Campbell.[3] These resources will help you formulate specific action plans for meeting the emotional needs of your children.

SUMMARY

To recognize the special needs of your kids, follow these principles:

Let your child be a normal child.

Recognize that kids are the most durable things God ever made.

Beware of men who want to spend excessive time alone with your children.

The next chapter will help you learn how to accept parenting realities.

SIX

Accepting the Realities of Parenting

"I'm spread so thin as a single mother that I don't feel I'm doing a good job at anything," Susan told me several years ago. "I come home from a hectic day at the bank and face yardwork and kids who need immediate attention. Later there's the checkbook to balance and priorities to establish for the week or month. I never seem to be caught up. Many times I feel totally overwhelmed."

Could I have quoted you saying these words? I'm happy to report that today, Susan's cup overflows. Her oldest daughter has a good job and is making a significant contribution to society. Her second daughter is married and establishing her own home. But how did Susan face parenting realities during her daughters' growing up years? How can single moms do the best job possible for their kids under such demanding circumstances?

THE REALITY OF STABILIZING

Can the single parent ever hope to provide her children with normal parenting? Yes, but much of it is contingent upon her own stabilization as a person.

The faster the single mom can stabilize her SELF (spiritually, emotionally, lovingly, financially), the faster she will be able to provide stronger parenting input for her children. The new family unit will probably never be a perfect "10," but the single mom and her network can come close to providing what's needed to prevent significant long-term damage. (And single moms always must remind themselves that their unbroken family unit wasn't a perfect "10" either—nor is any family in this hurting world.)

Single moms can be effective if they can be there for the children when they need her. The biggest decision many single moms face is whether to go to work or try to get by on the welfare and child-support (when it's paid). You may, for example, be able to go to work for a couple of thousand dollars a year more than you'd get on welfare, but an eight-hour work day plus commuting time takes a major chunk out of the day.

And a couple of thousand more is what most single moms will get—certainly if they have a junior college education or less. Our economic structure, with its low minimum wage, makes it almost impossible for a single parent to exceed welfare support without a college degree. (That's why I recommend you pursue a college degree once you have achieved initial stabilization.)

Jackie chose to return to school while whe was on AFDC and became a radiology technician. Her son was supported emotionally during this time with a strong set of grandparents. Jackie kept her spiritual focus and after four long years is working in a hospital and living on her own.

Sometimes, however, school can become an escape and turn into a problem. Phylis was driven to get a master's degree in counseling, and she allowed this goal to destroy her children. To keep up in school she chose to drop out of church and spend Sundays with her children. I counseled her to stay with her spiritual commitment and not to leave the church. Her response was that time spent with her children was more important than the church.

Five years later, Phylis was a licensed counselor—but one of her children was involved in drugs, another in witchcraft, and the oldest had committed suicide.

Single mothers need to keep the same priorities as everyone else: God, family, job, and ministry. Can it be done? Yes—yet the road is not an easy one, especially if you have several children.

THE REALITY OF DOLLARS AND CENTS

Because entry-level income is so low in the United States, today's welfare income exceeds what most single parents with a low education and undeveloped skills can earn. It's unrealistic for a single mother to hire a baby-sitter and go to work long-term at a minimum wage. The Census Survey reports that 50 percent of single moms work and the other 50 percent stay home with the kids. Unless you have a good marketable job skill or higher education, the wages may not be worth leaving the kids.

Because of this scenario, more and more single parents are opting to stay on welfare and be there for their children, especially once they realize this income is tax-free. In addition, they receive food stamps and medical and dental coverage. There's no doubt that the stigma of being on welfare can be painful, but in many cases this is the best choice for the children.

The Question of Where to Work

If you choose to work, one occupation that works well (at least until more education and experience are gained) is to waitress in daytime restaurants. Working a daytime shift will allow you to be at home most of the time when the children are at home. And the extra earning from tips can make this more rewarding financially.

The majority of mothers today are working even when married, so when the divorce comes they may have a career in place. My advice is not to change jobs in the midst of turmoil if you can help it.

Women who have a college degree have a better chance of earning a more acceptable income. Many single moms, for example, go into teaching, especially in states like California, where they can teach while upgrading their own education. Teaching provides a schedule that closely matches their children's. This largely solves the baby-sitting problem, or the latchkey child problem, because if you're working late the child can stay with you at school.

Another advantage of teaching is that it will put you in contact with children from dual-parent homes. This will help erase the perception that 80 percent of your own children's problems are because you're a single parent. You'll see kids from single-parent homes who are doing better than some of those from dual-parent homes.

The Advantages of Job Flexibility

Many single moms gravitate into the medical profession, some becoming vocational nurses, much like my mother did years ago. Others may become dental assistants or receptionists in medical offices (though at that level the pay is only marginally better than the income from welfare).

If you've had experience as a secretary you may find

a job that is not forty hours a week. More and more offices are accommodating skilled single moms because reliable, skilled secretaries are normally in short supply.

Other jobs where you can adjust hours to meet children's needs are as a checkout cashier in a supermarket or in telemarketing sales, where commissions or bonuses can really increase the take-home pay.

THE REALITY OF EXTRA DEMANDS

Can a single parent be an effective parent? Absolutely! I've seen it work countless times. When a single mom has stabilized her life and is available for the children when they really need her, she can provide 80 percent of the parenting a child would normally receive in a two-parent family. And I'll say it again—two-parent families don't have it all together either.

Right now you may be thinking, "Hold it! My kid's sneaking around and cutting school, and he erases the answering machine before I come home at night if a phone call comes from school. He knows when to intercept the mail with his progress report in it. As far as I'm concerned, that indicates a real failure as a parent." Wrong—these are experiences that my wife and I have had with our children.

This kind of story is why I try to get single parents I know into a regular home Bible studies after about a year. There they will hear the same horror stories from dual parents who are both working hard at their roles as parents. And gradually single moms will believe me when I say, "If you will take the emotional energy you were applying to maintaining your relationship with your husband and expend it on behalf of your child, you can actually make more progress than many two-parent families."

Here's another reason why I recommend that a single mom very seriously consider staying single during the growing-up years of her child. Single moms must deal with the reality of extra demands. Instead of expending so much energy on a relationship with a man, and adding even more demands on top of what's already there, the energy can flow into the relationships with her children.

How do you compensate for the extra demands on you? One way is to try some of the parenting seminars in your area in order to improve your parenting skills.

"Hold it," you say. "Those seminars are full of *couples*—I'll stick out like a sore thumb!"

Yes, it may be too tough an environment while you're still struggling with emotional control. But if you're becoming more stabilized, and perhaps have been interacting with couples in a Bible study, you will find parenting seminars extremely useful. Not only will you learn a lot from the lectures, you will find other parents eager to share insights with you. And if you look for them, you'll probably find other single parents at these seminars, too.

Single parents have told me that you can learn some things at parenting seminars for couples that you will not get at single-parenting seminars.

If you feel really awkward attending events that seem to shout "couples only," why not consider teaming up with another single mom? Sharing a hotel room can be fun and economical. Or two families could share facilities at a family conference at a camp. Two moms and three or four kids can live together in a cabin and just flow right into what is going on.

Handling the Other Twenty Percent
So how do you deal with the 20 percent of parenting that is very difficult to provide in the single-parent home?

The number one issue is *supervision*: being able to provide the authority structure and proper attention your children need. And that clearly depends on the number of hours you are able to be around your children. If your children have a baby-sitter or are placed in group child-care for most of the day, then you're sharing supervision with others. This doesn't have to be a negative situation, but you'll have to work harder to make sure the supervision is acceptable to you. (Check with local churches and other single mothers for references. The issues are protection, supervision, and training.)

Your kids may try to exploit any lack of supervision to their advantage. But children from a two-parent home, where both parents are working, will do the same thing.

The second issue single moms struggle with a lot is adult male influence. Some activities are more typically male, like fishing and hunting. I suggested earlier that father substitutes may need to be carefully found for some of these activities through the church, Scouts, and other organizations. But creative single moms may be able to involve their children in these activities without adult men.

I was fascinated when two single moms teamed up to buy camping equipment. The families drove to a park, put up a tent, and camped. The women weren't experienced at it (since their ex-husbands did not camp with them anyway), but they just went ahead and did it anyway. They scrounged around, got wet and dirty, and had a lot of fun. This kind of adventure meant leaving their comfort zone and stretching their skills, but the effort paid off.

The worst scenario is when the single mom gets into a relationship with a male single parent just to get a father for her boys . . . only to find he'll take only his *own* kids when he goes fishing or camping. Now you're really in trouble with your kids!

The third issue in handling the other 20 percent of parenting is your child's lack of a dual perspective on the world. Single moms may be so taxed with just keeping the household functioning that they don't have time to keep up with much of what is going on in the rest of the world.

Here you may need to make extra effort to meet the extra demands. I know single moms who read the sports pages every day, who can spout box scores and list key players' abilities with the most avid men. They make an effort to do it to keep in touch with their sons through interests and hobbies.

A fourth issue in the extra demands of single parenting is that children lack a "court of appeal." When the edict comes down from mom—"This is the way it is going to be"—children have no one else in the home to appeal to. They've lost the man who may have understood their particular concerns or wishes in a way that mom doesn't. That gets real, real frustrating. I know, because I was there!

When I was twelve I wanted a BB gun, but my mom said no. The issue of guns and weapons is appalling to many women. If I had had a father who hunted, I could have appealed to him for moral support at least. Without that support I chose to solve the issue myself, and stole a BB gun from a hardware store. As a very new Christian I knew it was wrong, but I wanted the gun.

In the months that followed I became careless with it and got into BB gun wars with other kids. The end result is that I was shot in the eye and almost blinded. Over the years I've come to realize that in that incident God took over as Father in my life and disciplined me over the rebellion against my mother and the theft of the gun.

Janet was raised by a single father who was very firm in his discipline, but occasionally failed to express interest in her "female" needs. After a heated discussion over makeup when Janet was sixteen, it was her father's girlfriend who was able to appeal to him for a compromise between the "painted lady" and the "pale face."

SUMMARY

Keep these parenting realities in mind:

Your time and presence are more valuable than money.

The best job is one that flexes with your children.

Your children need some court of appeal.

Accepting the realities of parenting doesn't have to mean just gritting your teeth and gutting it out. In some areas, you can make surprising progress. But there will always be those times when it's just plain difficult. In fact, in the next chapter we'll explore how God Himself knows what it's like to be the frustrated parent. You're not alone in accepting the realities of parenting—you're in great company!

SEVEN

God Understands the Frustrated Parent

Policemen never get over the emotional horror of the scene: A parent who kills all the children and then takes his or her own life. And as you read the report in the newspaper you say to yourself or a friend, "I can't imagine anyone ever getting *that* frustrated about caring for their children."

It *is* hard to imagine. But I've seen many single parents, and even those in a dual-parent family, get really close to that level of violence. In fact, I think most parents have wished at one time or another that their kids just didn't exist. (Have you heard the one about the kid who said he never asked to be born? Good thing you didn't, the parent answered—I'd have said No!)

The Bible tells us that God Himself once wiped out all but eight people and another time threatened to do it again. So maybe those feelings we have are not that abnormal.

What is it that triggers those kinds of overwhelming, frustrated feelings in a parent, especially a single parent?

GOD, THE FRUSTRATED BUT MERCIFUL PARENT

To start our search for understanding frustration, let's look back at the time of Noah:

> Then the LORD saw that the wickedness of man was great on the earth, and that every intent of the thoughts of his heart was only evil continually. (Genesis 6:5)

Ever felt like that was the condition of your kids? I know I have! So what's your response in that situation? Consider how God felt:

> And the LORD was sorry that He made man on the earth, and He was grieved in His heart. And the LORD said, "I will blot out man whom I have created from the face of the land, from man to animals to creeping things and to birds of the sky; for I am sorry that I have made them." (Genesis 6:6-7)

This is the voice of a frustrated parent. God had given the people of that day opportunity after opportunity, and they had wasted every one. They had gone their own way, openly rebelling against the authority and loving guidance of their Creator.

Some years after Noah's death, Moses and Aaron were leading the Israelites in the wilderness after their miraculous release from bondage in Egypt. God had destroyed the Egyptians as they pursued Israel, and again demonstrated that He cared for the Israelites by providing water and food. To help them deal with freedom and develop a national identity, He gave them a whole code of laws, summed up in the Ten Commandments. He communicated these laws to Moses on Mount Sinai.

But when Moses did not come down from the mountain for forty days, the Israelites figured he was a goner. Without delay they reverted to the pattern of idolatry practiced in Egypt and ended up dancing around a golden calf while engaging in all kinds of sinful revelry.

God did not take kindly to this backsliding by Israel:

> Then the LORD spoke to Moses, "Go down at once, for your people, whom you brought up from the land of Egypt, have corrupted themselves. They have quickly turned away from the way which I commanded them. They have made for themselves a molten calf, and have worshiped it, and have sacrificed to it and said, 'This is your god, O Israel, who brought you up from the land of Egypt!' And the LORD said to Moses, 'I have seen this people, and behold, they are an obstinate people. Now then let Me alone, that My anger may burn against them, and that I may destroy them; and I will make of you a great nation.'" (Exodus 32:7-10)

Doesn't that sound like a frustrated parent who has given up on the effectiveness of discipline?

The whole process of redeeming His people from sin is frustrating to God—just as single parenting often is for us. In fact, it is more so, since God could control everything if He really wanted to, and we cannot. He could clamp down and turn us into robots, which we cannot do with our children, even though there are times we wish our kids *were* robots.

But God is unwilling to wipe out His offspring, and so He has resorted to all sorts of discipline. From our perspective, He must often have said, "What do I do next to keep this people of mine in line?"

A remarkable feature of God as a parent is His recurring grace and mercy just when He seems to have reached the end of His rope. King David knew all about that, for after he covered up his affair with Bathsheba by having her husband, Uriah the Hittite, killed, God responded to David's repentance and restored Him to fellowship. That's why David could exclaim:

> The LORD is compassionate and gracious, slow to anger and abounding in lovingkindness. He will not always strive with us; nor will he keep His anger forever. He has not dealt with us according to our sins, nor rewarded us according to our iniquities. (Psalm 103:8-10)

God's willingness to forgive is most reassuring to single parents who typically take on too much responsibility for the way their children eventually will turn out. As a single parent, you are not solely responsible for your child's ultimate development. Children make their own decisions—just as Israel did in turning to idolatry, just as David did in committing adultery. And when your child makes wrong decisions there may be discipline, but there should also always be love and mercy as well, just as Israel and David experienced from God.

Let's look at a few key issues in disciplining children.

WHEN MANIPULATION CORNERS YOU

Just as God experienced genuine frustration with the first humans, Adam and Eve, who set a pattern of rebellion and self-will that still exists, so parents quickly recognize that their children are Adam's descendants. It takes about twenty minutes after birth; from that point on children learn to use you and your emotions for their own benefit.

I'll admit it's easier for two parents to deal with this manipulation. One parent may be able to provide some objectivity while the other is being emotionally manipulated. If you are parenting alone you will not have this kind of early warning system for manipulative advances.

I find single parents most susceptible to a child's manipulation right after separation or divorce, while they're immersed in the overwhelming feelings of alienation. Sometimes kids will take advantage of this. They can really zero in and split the seams between parents who are no longer together. There is so much energy going into the battle between the parents that the kids can get away with "murder."

What are the frustrating realities that challenge the single parent in the case of manipulation? First there is the intensity and the wildness of the hostility that you may be experiencing in relationship to your ex. You may still be swinging through wild surges of rage in a full-blown hostility that you have never experienced before. And you're probably very frustrated by it, especially if you kept yourself under tight control up to that time.

This rage has a way of spilling over into your interaction with the children. You simply are unable to cope normally with their actions. As a result you begin to strike out at them verbally and even physically, something you rarely, or never, did before the divorce—and you hate yourself for it. But it happens, and you seem powerless to control it because of the intensity of your anger.

The scenarios vary, but in many cases the child will

begin to yell back at you, something that may never have happened before. She is just as frustrated with the change in the family environment as you are, so she yells at you. And you yell back . . . and can't believe it's your voice. But it is, and you're *so frustrated!* This leads us into another area of frustration: dealing with your own anger.

WHEN ANGER LEAPS OUT OF CONTROL

A classic parenting frustration is trying to get children to do something that they just won't do. You ask your son to wash the dishes or clean up his room, and all you get is stonewalling, resistance, or outright defiance.

So you lose your temper and strike out in anger, something you had been able to control within a dual-parent environment where at worst there was intervention. Now without someone to modulate your anger, you begin throwing things. (Remember the steps of destruction back in chapter 2?)

This particularly becomes a problem during the thawing-out period, when you're not yet in command of yourself and your emotions. During this time, losing control is a real problem. This is apparently because now is when you really want to get at your husband, but you can't. So you end up taking it out on the kids, often without realizing it.

God measured out discipline in sound doses, but the single mom does not have anything near that level of control for some time. There are times when she will give her child total freedom but put the hammer down the very next minute. Or she might just turn the child loose for a few days. During these times she vacillates between super-loose and super-severe, which leaves the child totally frustrated, too.

A FATHER'S HELP FOR THE FATHERLESS

Besides His grace and mercy and experience as a heavenly parent, what does God provide for the single parent?

God has committed Himself to being a Father to the fatherless. Psalm 68:5 declares, "A father of the fatherless and a judge for the widows, is God in His holy habitation." Throughout the Bible He demonstrates a special concern for the fatherless and the widows.

Yet what kind of God is this Father to the fatherless? Many of us have a distorted view of God because we see Him through the lense of our earthly fathers. But that is not the God we find in the Bible, for He is all-loving, He is totally consumed with meeting our needs, and He really cares for us as individuals.

The God who has promised to be a Father to the fatherless is a concrete example of one parent with unconditional love and discipline. He provides direction without being overbearing. He disciplines, but He is not harshly punitive. And the warm, intimate love relationship He has with us as individuals is what He desires us to have with our own children.

In my experience, God has a very loving and tender heart for the children of single parents. He gives special attention to children and widows, those who are doing without, who are hurting emotionally and having to suffer.

I believe that God has given me special abilities, opportunities, and protection simply because I was raised by a single parent. At the same time His vision for my life was beyond my wildest expectations. I never believed that I would be able to go even to junior college. Yet by God's grace I finished a B.A., M.A., and Ph.D. This is just one of the commitments I feel God made to me as the child of a single mom.

Another commitment He brings to the environment of single-parent families is that He will bless those single parents and children who follow Him—in a way that differs from how He blesses those from a two-parent home. For example, I'm convinced that my desire for a ministry focused on single parents grew out of my experience of pain as the oldest in a single parent home. Through that background God gave me a sensitivity to care for those who are in a similar situation. I really believe I probably wouldn't have just these qualities if I'd grown up in a "normal" two-parent home. To me this has been a great blessing, for it has led me to a rewarding career of helping others.

THE BENEFITS OF PAIN

I try to explain to single moms that there are some real benefits of experiencing single-parent family struggles.

For example, young men can gain a deeper understanding of life and what it means to grow up when they have to take on responsibility prematurely—such as in having to stand up for and defend his home, in doing some things around the home, and in contributing some or all of all his income to support the family.

I discovered early on that some material things in life are not that important. I did not get a high school graduation picture because I just didn't have the money. Nor could I afford a class ring. Now it was my choice whether to be bitter about it—which I was for a while—or to recognize it as God's way of preparing me for ministry. There is a lot of pain and agony in ministry.

If I had come out of a stable, hard-driving family, a really powerful family that provided me with a lot of financial resources, I don't think I could be functioning as I do today. But since I did not have many possessions growing up, I don't expect a lot now. That attitude has served me well: I'm happy with what I have.

So when you hit your frustration threshold in being a single parent, with children who are disobedient and seem to be drifting away from you, remember that's how God has felt many times about His rebellious children. But He has committed Himself to helping you make it as a single parent. He has a redemptive plan for you and your family.

GOD'S REDEMPTIVE PLAN

After Adam and Eve had disobeyed God's express command not to eat of the tree of the knowledge of good and evil, their frustrated parent, God, exercised firm discipline. But in the midst of those events He had important purposes at work. When He told the serpent, "I will put enmity between you and the woman, and between your seed and her seed; He shall bruise you on the head, And you shall bruise him on the heel" (Genesis 3:15), it was an early hint of the coming crucifixion of Jesus. Even the banishment from the Garden of Eden had good results, for it prevented Adam and Eve from eating of the tree of life.

God's redemptive purposes with humanity were demonstrated many times in that great father of the Hebrew nation, Abraham. We hold him up as a model of faith, but twice he misrepresented who his wife Sarai was, referring to her as his sister. Each time God rescued him by communicating directly with the ruler who had taken Sarai into his harem, instead of exercising harsh discipline.

Looking at it from the human perspective, it's clear that it didn't take God long to figure out that He was going to have as much trouble with His children as we have with ours. Some of them were going to be obedient; some were going to rebel. But He never gave up on His plan for redemption.

SUMMARY

If God is this interested in the redemption of the human family, and in the well-being of you and your children in particular, then you can have hope and peace in the midst of the most frustrating realities.

Remember these lessons to reduce frustration in parenting:

God had His parenting problems, just like everyone else.

Consistent and firm discipline combined with love is enough.

"When all you can do, is all you can do, then all you can do is enough!" (A. L. Williams).

How can you and your family turn toward God, rather than away from Him? In the next chapter we'll focus on establishing the right priorities for building spiritual vitality in your kids.

EIGHT

Building Spiritual Vitality in Your Kids

I t's evening. The sounds of the day have died down. You're about to leave your child's bedroom after giving the window shade one last tug to make sure the street light doesn't shine in. The faint glow of the night light in the bathroom guides your steps.

You look back a final time at the tousled head on the pillow as memories of the day flood your mind. In the morning you made sure she received a good breakfast and left for school with a full lunch box. When she returned you were ready with milk and a cookie. You listened as she told about the day's adventures at school, then went back to your household tasks while she ran out to play with the neighborhood kids.

You served a carefully balanced dinner of green leafy vegetables, carrots, potatoes, and chicken. After eating you watched a television show together, then read a bedtime story. And you listened as she talked to God through her favorite prayers.

As your glance lingers on your child's sleeping form you wonder: What is the most important thing I can do to be sure she grows up a balanced person who loves God and others?

Of course, it's not only single parents who ask themselves this question. Children in dual-parent homes face the same pressures, but there is the implicit feeling that their chances of becoming balanced adults who love and serve God are much better than those of children raised by single parents. And you probably worry a lot more than the parent in a dual-parent family because you consider yourself solely responsible, especially if your ex is not a good influence.

What can you do to reduce the worry level and increase the chances of success? Let's go back to the concept of God as a Father to the fatherless.

GOD CARES

God, the one who sent His Son, Jesus Christ, to die in your place so you could be released from the penalty of sin, also had your children in mind when He told us through the psalmist that He is "a father of the fatherless and a judge for the widows" (Psalm 68:5).

You may not be in partnership with a husband in bringing up your children, but you can be in partnership with the Almighty God of the universe. He's the one who has counted the hairs on your head and numbered your days. His love will never fail. And each moment of every day He knows where you are, what your needs are. He's also aware of your children as they catch a bus for school, play on the school grounds, and take classes with a teacher you don't know.

Reassuring? You bet it is, if you will learn to rest in Him and trust His judgment. This assurance that God cares for your children leads to a second step you can take.

GOD HEARS OUR PRAYERS

Maybe you've heard the stories about mothers whose faithful prayers for their children had a major impact on the children's lives. There's one about a man living on the streets who finally surrenders to Jesus Christ and exclaims, "The memory of a praying mother followed me every day even when I was far away from God. How I wish I could let her know that God has answered her prayer!"

These stories may have seemed a bit melodramatic when you heard them, but the reality is that *God has promised to answer our prayers.* Jesus put it very simply and directly: "All things you ask in prayer, believing, you shall receive" (Matthew 21:22).

Maybe you wonder a bit about that word *believing,* since at this point your faith seems to be rather small. Then think for a minute about something else Jesus said: "If you have faith as a mustard seed, you shall say to this mountain, 'Move from here to there,' and it shall move; and nothing shall be impossible to you" (Matthew 17:20).

That's tremendously reassuring for any of us with little faith, for it isn't our faith that moves mountains—it's God's power. Even so, as we pray for the emotional, physical, and spiritual well-being of our children, it's not our faith, but God's ability to accomplish it that will make it happen.

One of the single moms I know prays every day for each of her children. She asks God for four things:

1. That they will spiritually walk with the Lord.
2. That they will make the right kinds of friends.
3. That they will meet and look up to the right kinds of adults.
4. That they will find and marry a godly mate.

That kind of focused praying meets the Apostle Paul's criteria that "in all things with prayer and supplication" we should present our requests to the heavenly Father.

In fact, I've reached the conclusion that the single parent has a leg up on dual parents in this whole matter of prayer. Prayer reveals our dependence upon God and, unfortunately, a lot of dual parents depend on each other far more than they depend upon God. But single parents often feel they have no one except God to turn to, so they pray a lot more, and learn to depend upon God for more. That dependence can bring hope and assurance.

FINDING TIME FOR SPIRITUAL NURTURE

Time for prayer and reading the Word of God is often tough for single moms. Yet it doesn't have to be a big thing. Single moms occasionally get all hung up because they don't have a formal time for personal Bible reading and prayer seven days a week—after all, that's what the truly spiritual people do, don't they? I say to them, "So start with twice a week. Set your goal at that. Be happy and content." And remember that you can shoot quick prayers to God no matter where you are or what you're doing.

One of the single moms I know leaves for her lunch break at 11:30 when the lunchroom is still deserted. For the next thirty minutes she has her personal time with the Lord, reading the Bible and praying.

One single dad has an hour's ride to work. For the first half hour he has to concentrate all his attention on traffic, but after that he has a stretch through the desert that permits him to focus on praising the Lord and presenting his needs.

Do you realize what a direct result this has on your

children? Remember, *kids learn more by your consistent doing than by your mouthing of spiritual language.*

MODELING DEPENDENCE ON GOD

The greatest legacy you can leave your children, the attitude and activity that will impact your children more than anything else, is *modeling total dependence on God*. And for single parents this tends to comes a lot easier than for dual parents, because they don't need anyone else's permission or approval.

A single mom who is walking with God and having to depend upon God for wisdom, for direction, and for provision of daily needs, models direct contact with the Almighty. She is not dependent upon a man to meet her needs, nor does she look first to other resources.

If the single mom will let her kids experience this dependence upon God with her, it will transfer into a similar dependence upon God in their life. Remember: one of your primary goals of parenting is to raise your children to be godly parents who will raise your grandchildren in the way of the Lord.

In my case, I was just blown away at how much my mom was able to depend upon the Lord as she raised four kids, spent two years at college, got her vocational nursing license, and went to work in the hospital. More than that, I was overwhelmed by her walk with the Lord on an everyday basis, and by the support she received from the people in our little church.

And it was a *tiny* church. If we had forty people on Sunday, we thought that revival had come. Yet that little church put its arms around my mother and helped her make it through not only the first few weeks after my dad left, but the years afterward as she raised the four of us.

THE IMPORTANCE OF CHURCH

Beyond faith in God's care for your children, praying regularly for them, and modeling dependence on God, what else can you do that will provide direction and spiritual support for your children? *Take them to church.*

I am absolutely convinced that for your children to "turn out right," the spiritual dimension has to take priority, and that means taking your children to church. The younger they are when you start, the better. You cannot send them—you need to go there with them.

Children in a single-parent home primarily have one role model to whom they look for guidance in life. If that one adult in their life is not doing something (like attending church), who else will model that commitment?

This is especially true of a single mom raising boys. Young men are harder to influence later on when they get into their teens, when peer pressure is at its worst. That's when they need a quality peer group at church. If you do not provide that peer group, they will, and you will probably not be comfortable with some of their choices.

Frankly, I consider keeping your children in a good church with a good youth group the best parenting insurance you can have. I recommend even passing up a work promotion if that takes you away from the church where your children have established peer relationships. Once you're in a church where your kids are a functioning part of a group peer structure, especially in junior and senior high, protect it above all else.

In my twenty years with singles I have many times seen the devastation when single parents disrupt Christian peer relationships developed in church youth groups. Once that connection is broken in junior or senior high school, the influence of the world often seems to overwhelm young people and carry them away from God.

This consequence occurs when you move to a new church and your children find it hard to break into the youth group circles. The new peer groups they subsequently form will normally be nonChristian. And once loyalties have shifted away from church peer groups it is very, very hard to get them back.

Obviously, there are times when you simply *have* to change churches. My wife and I experienced that in our family. But we did everything we could to reestablish our kids quickly in a new youth group where they could develop new peer relationships with Christians.

Over and over single parents ask me, "Do I have to make my kids go to church when they don't want to?" It can be a hassle, especially when kids are in junior or senior high school. And parents feel it really isn't worth the battle Sunday after Sunday.

I ask them, "Do you make them brush they teeth?" Usually they say yes. Then I ask, "Why do you make them do that?" And they respond, "I don't want them to have any cavities." I reply, "Then you also need to bring them to church on Sunday so they will not have spiritual cavities. If you don't bring them, I can guarantee they will have spiritual cavities. You can take them to a dentist and find out in a hurry if they haven't been brushing their teeth—and you pay for it. You're going to pay a lot more in emotional energy if you let your kids develop spiritual cavities, because you might not discover them for years—after it's too late."

Years ago I heard a great personal example from Dr. Henry Brandt, the Christian psychologist. He said that his children constantly needed help to get to church. "I had to help them get dressed," he said," and sometimes I had to carry them screaming into the car. But an amazing thing took place when I got to church and opened the car door. They did not need any help to go play with their friends at church . . . but it took a lot of effort to get them there." Make the effort—get your kids to church!

Younger children offer you the opportunity to ingrain spiritual and moral values into their young lives with minimal effort. Start young and be consistent. The longer you wait, the harder it is and the more energy it takes.

A final word of caution: One of the worst things parents can do is gripe about their church. A lot of parents have turned their kids off because of constant complaining about the church at home. They gripe about the pastor, about how the church is hurting them, about something at the board level. And the kids see the church as hurting their parents, and they want no part of anything that hurts their parents.The situation is magnified in a single parent family. Your children will normally have tremendous loyalty to you. When you gripe about the treatment you have received from the pastor or from the church, you make the children take sides. And they will take sides with you against the church. So don't be surprised later if they don't want to go to the church you've been complaining about. Model positive attitudes about your church.

REINFORCING BIBLICAL VALUES

Even with a good youth group your child still needs spiritual reinforcement at home. God instructed Israel to make spiritual instruction a priority in the home:

> And these words, which I am commanding you
> today, shall be on your heart; and you shall teach
> them diligently to your sons and shall talk of
> them when you sit in your house and when you

walk by the way and when you lie down and when you rise up. (Deuteronomy 6:6-7)

So what can the busy single parent do? Despite what you may think, don't sweat it! Notice the method of communicating truth that God commanded to Israel. In our western culture we so easily translate spiritual instruction into regimented teaching, but what God suggests is *a lifestyle of communicating His truth.*

The fact is that *values are more caught than taught.* Your consistent dependence upon God, as expressed in prayer and as you converse with your children, is more important than whether they have devotions every day (as valuable as these can be if they are not "ram it down, cram it down" sessions).

For example, take time at supper to discuss the day's happenings in the light of how God wants us to live. Let your children share what they have experienced, and when appropriate, frame these in the context of God's love and care for us.

Again this is one of the advantages for the single parent who does not have to interact with a husband. She can focus all her energy on the children and very deliberately involve them in ongoing interaction based on biblical principles.

This does get harder to do when a single mom goes to work and has much less time with her children. That's why many women struggle with whether to get a job or stay home on welfare. The kids need all of you they can get, at least while they're young and in their most impressionable years. That time at home can really establish a set of life values that will stand your children in good stead for the rest of their lives.

Auxiliary, or "in-home," employment is an option

I have seen work. Three single parents I know operate home child-care centers. That gets them off welfare and receiving regular income, but it also permits them to stay at home and be around for their kids at all times.

MAKING THE BEST USE OF HOME BASE

You've resolved the issue of praying for your children. You take time to talk with them about God and how He is at work in the world and in your lives today. You are committed to modeling dependence upon God for everything. You've got your kids in a good youth group with positive peer pressure, and you even send them to camp for a more intensive experience with Christian kids and leaders. Anything else you can do? Yes—make the best use of home base.

Some of the single moms I know are practicing hospitality even though they have few financial resources. They're willing to share what they have with other families, especially those with positive male role models and sons near the age of their own. They recognize the value of building these kinds of relationships with other families who honor God.

In addition to reaching out to other families, you can take the initiative to have other kids visit in your home. That's better than letting your kids wander off into other homes, where you don't know what they're getting into. This is a particular tendency with boys. Use your home as a base by providing a hospitable environment for the kids in your neighborhood and friends from school.

SUMMARY

Here are the most important principles in building spiritual vitality in your kids:

Live a godly life as a model for your children.

Take your children to church, even if they complain. It's easier to deal with resentment than spiritual ignorance.

Support your local church. Don't gripe about it in front of your kids.

It's not simple or easy to establish a home in which Jesus Christ is honored and loved. But the rewards make it all worthwhile, especially when you see your children developing into well-balanced adults who love the Lord and serve Him gladly.

NINE

Knowing When You're Ready for Another Relationship

W hat's the most dangerous period of the single parent's life? When do you need a same-sex friend who can be honest with you more than at any other time?

Believe it or not, *it's when you start healing*—when your emotional energy is coming back, when you have enough mental concentration to start reading a book again.

"You're putting me on," you think. But I'm not. As soon as you start getting better you think you're okay. You're thawing out, and the hurt has subsided. You feel in control. Forget the five-year healing period. You're ready for another relationship!

No—hold on. Let's take a closer look.

Once a man begins to show you focused attention, *watch out*. This is the first warning light that should catch your attention. Instead of pursuing the relationship, you need to slow down, stay in a group setting, and play it cool.

Why? Because although you feel much better, *you still have a lot of rebuilding to do*. You still need to regain more self-esteem, increase your spiritual maturity, and get your moral defenses in better shape. And there's also the issue of energy.

We looked at a chart in chapter 2 (see figure 3 on pages 28-29) that shows the effects of divorce on your emotional, physical, mental, and spiritual energy levels. When totally healthy, you may have 25 percent of your energy supply invested in emotional energy.

However, six months or so after the divorce, when it seems that your recovery is really underway, the emotional drain is still channeling off most of your energy. You may have only five to 10 percent invested in other areas, which means that for the most part your emotional dimension exerts great power over your phsical, mental, and spiritual aspects. Your feelings may tell you that you have a lot more capacity in these other areas, but remember: your feelings are deceptive.

THE POWER OF NEED

Let's assume you've reached the 10 percent mark in the other areas. Now, 70 percent of your energy is going to meet emotional needs. Enter the attractive man on your horizon, who zooms in on you. You're not only flattered, but excited. This man meets some needs that you thought had died during and after the divorce. Your sexuality is awakened. *Beware, you are extremely vulnerable.*

Why are you in danger?

First, *you gain a level of acceptance in this relationship that is so new and exciting that you feel it must be right.* How could it be wrong when it feels so right? Not even your husband accepted you the way this man does. And after feeling rejected by your ex for so long, you crave acceptance. Wanting acceptance is normal; it's the *kind* of acceptance that's the issue. It must be authentic.

But the man's attention seems to spark a whole new personality in you. You begin to develop a new vision of yourself and gain new self-worth because someone considers you valuable. You start to dress differently, talk excitedly, and truly feel that you're a new person. And it's all because of the new man in your life.

It's only normal that you want to protect this new relationship. After all, guys like this don't come by every day. In fact, you begin to think, *there may never be another one like him.* So you cling on, no matter what, regardless of what it costs you, and in spite of what anyone—maybe even God—has to say about it.

DOWN THE ENERGY DRAIN

Life is starting to feel different, and you like it. But wait—you're still a single parent, aren't you? The kids still need you to put them to bed, wake them up in the morning, make sure they're ready for school, and feed them when they come home. You need energy to do all that, but you're using it up elsewhere.

Relationships suck up a lot of energy, especially for the single parent. Since you may not have been involved emotionally with someone of the opposite sex for a long time, your relational skills may have atrophied. They're just not what they used to be. In particular, your moral resistance skills may still be too weak to meet the demands on them.

It's like getting behind the wheel again after going for a long time without driving a car. You tend to step on the gas too hard, then stomp on the brake to compensate, almost getting whiplash in the process. It takes a while for you to regain the skills to operate a car smoothly. And in the process you burn up a lot of energy. Fear, excitement, and stress have a way of doing that.

Ditto for your new relationship. You tend to move too quickly, just to lock in the relationship, giving the man more than he really is asking for initially. Then you get scared, so you pull back. Suddenly you think you're in danger of losing him, so you go full speed ahead again.

What does this do to your energy level? It opens up a drain to send your energy down. But you didn't have much energy to begin with, and so whatever you're putting into the new relationship has to come from somewhere—probably from what you'd been giving to your children. You may actually be drawing energy from them to support you in your new relationship.

What does this do to your kids? They lose the energy input from you, or at least that's the way it seems. Before you met your man, they were anxious to get a new dad. They had talked a lot about finding someone for you. (Or was it for them?) Now that you have this exciting new relationship they should be happy, right? Wrong—they turn sour, resentful, angry. You can't figure it out.

Here's what has happened. As you became more healthy the kids were getting help and attention from you at your increased energy level. It was great—they loved it; it was just what they needed. After all, they hadn't gotten much real attention during the first few months of your healing process.

Now, however, your energy is going to this other person. The new man in your life is getting more than his fair share. Without fail, your kids will resent it. In fact, they will fight it. They will become more negative, drag their feet, and express more and more resistance. Once you get all of your energy back, it's another ballgame, but until that happens they won't be supportive of your new relationship.

The kids' resentment drains you of whatever reserve you have, further weakening your awareness of what is going on in your relationship.

TOO CLOSE TOO SOON

What should tip you off that there's real danger in your new relationship? The easiest warning sign to notice is *how much time you spend together*. When you start seeing this special person, keep a brief record of how many hours you're together each week. When the time starts to increase dramatically, watch out. You're in the danger zone. You may need to slow down and spread out the time.

The second tip-off is the *length* of time you spend together during each date. If your man shows up and spends seven or eight hours a day with you, whether you do it at home or on the beach, it's too much time at this stage. That's especially true if you go away together for a weekend.

Friendships shouldn't require that much time. Relationships do. But if you're in too early a stage of your recovery you probably don't have the emotional energy to handle a rapidly developing, demanding relationship.

There used to be a television commercial in which many cars were lined up with all the lights turned on to see which one's battery would last the longest. Then drivers would get into the cars and try to start their engines. The engine with the winning battery turned over with a healthy roar; the others cranked away in futility.

Are you creating a drain on your battery? If you wait too long the lights may still be on, but there won't be enough power to restart the engine. At this stage in your healing process, developing a new relationship is drawing off current. You never know when you'll run out of moral battery power—leaving you without the energy to say no or run when you should run. The Bible tells us to "flee immorality" (1 Corinthians 6:18). You can't flee if you no longer have the energy to run.

THE WAY IT USUALLY HAPPENS

Although the following scenario does not happen to every single mom, it happens so often that I feel compelled to explain what occurs with too many newly-divorced women.

It all starts slowly and innocently enough. He calls for a dinner date. Next time a movie is added. Soon he's coming over after the movie to hold hands for a while. Then he drops by to help with the yardwork on Saturday . . . followed by boating on Sunday. By now there is more physical contact, kissing, hugging, and some petting (I define petting as touching parts on the other person's body that you do not have on your own). After a few weeks there's an invitation to spend a weekend at the lake.

Guess what happens at the lake? Premarital sex, which leads to guilt and a desire to make it right—marriage. Unfortunately, this is too often just another troubled relationship that results in a weak marriage . . . and the single mom starts all over again.

What people don't realize is that the energy needed to keep up that pace in building the relationship depletes the moral battery. And when the topic of going to bed comes up, there's not enough emotional energy left to say no.

The fact is that you never know when that time is going to come until you actually get there . . . and by

then it may be too late. The large chunk of time you gave
the relationship left you totally vulnerable.

THE PROBLEMS YOU CAN AVOID

The danger of getting into bed is not the only problem
in getting too close too soon. Let's look at the benefits of
staying out of a serious relationship at this stage in your
recovery process.

First, and possibly most important, *you will conserve
energy needed to speed your healing process.* Relationships
are hard work. Because they take a lot of energy from
you, they slow down the healing process. If you're not
well enough to deal with the stresses that come with the
new relationship, you can regress spiritually, emotionally, lovingly, and even financially.

A second benefit of critical importance to the single
parent is that *you will conserve time and energy needed to
give to your children.* They really need all the extra energy
you're getting as you begin to heal, since they've been
deprived for so long. On top of that, now is not the time to
let resentments toward you build up in them—you need
all the goodwill and love you can get.

A third benefit of avoiding serious relationships right
now is that *you won't risk getting burned by an unhealthy
relationship.* This means you're better prepared for healthy
relationships later on down the road. If that first relationship after divorce is not a good one, it will tend to recycle
you back into the old pattern of low self-esteem, anger,
and bitterness. You will tend also to go back to spending
time with the same kind of people you once felt comfortable with—hurting, angry, bitter people—instead of
moving into the circle of more mature and stable people
who have solid spiritual foundations.

AFTER IT HAPPENS—THEN WHAT?

Some single parents I know ran the moral battery down too far and couldn't say no when tempted to have sex. Afterward they were devastated by the fact that, while cautioning their own kids to stay moral in dating relationships, they had succumbed to temptation themselves.

Amazingly, this so often occurs when they had just begun to feel better and have energy for their kids. Everything was going great, God had been good to them, they had been stabilizing spiritually and emotionally, had rebuilt their relationship with their family, and even had a little extra money. They were thrilled at how well they were doing. Then they got sexually involved, and just crashed and burned.

Sometimes these single parents, feeling so bad about their behavior, will disappear from our singles ministry for six to eight months. Often they return in the pit of despair. Their kids usually have not been in church for six to eight months either, and sometimes they don't come back because, if they're in their teens, they have established a new peer group outside the church.

For the Christian single parent, once there is sexual contact—and that doesn't have to mean intercourse; fondling is included here—there is tremendous guilt, agony, pain, and frustration. This is true even in the "enlightened" nineties. The person is just recovering from relational trauma, and the guilt drives her down again spiritually and emotionally. She may try to pull away from the relationship, but the agony of being alone is so intense that she heads back.

The next step may be to get sexually involved at a more advanced level, and then a new dynamic takes over. The couple may have the feeling that they have committed a moral sin and cannot be forgiven. And because they have had a sexual relationship they must get married.

Trying to stop this process is like trying to grab a runaway train. The driving force overpowers all reasons not to marry. That drivenness is rooted in the "I'm trying to do what is right" philosophy, and "doing right" is interpreted as getting married after having had sex. So the first mistake—premarital sex—is compounded by a second mistake—marriage. The failure rate of second marriages is over 60 percent, according to the Census Survey. The single mom starts all over again, more devastated than before. Unfortunately, the more times you marry, the shorter each marriage tends to be.

But there *is* forgiveness for premarital sex. A hasty marriage is not the only possibility left after it happens.

When single parents caught up in an accelerating relationship come to me for counsel, I first ask them to indicate how far the relationship has advanced in physical intimacy. I ask them where they've been on a scale of one to ten, with each number corresponding to a level of contact, from look and touch through successive intensities of sexual expression leading to intercourse.

The Physical Scale of 1-10
1. Look
2. Touch
3. Lightly hold hands
4. Constantly hold hands
5. Light kiss
6. Strong kiss
7. French kiss
8. Fondle the breasts
9. Fondle the sexual organs
10. Sexual intercourse

My purpose in this initial step is to discover if sexual involvement is driving the relationship toward marriage. If there has been sexual contact, I want to deal with the guilt first and see if I can help the person view the sin in true biblical perspective. If we are able to do that, we can stall that drivenness toward marriage long enough to evaluate it properly.

Forgiveness for sexual sin is not only possible; it has already been offered. It is rooted in the redemption God accomplished when Jesus died in our place and took *all* of our sin on Him. Here's how Peter, the man who denied His Lord three times, proclaimed it: "He Himself bore our sins in His body on the cross, that we might die to sin and live to righteousness; for by His wounds you were healed" (1 Peter 2:24). If Peter could be forgiven, if the thief on the cross could be forgiven, if the "chief sinner," the Apostle Paul, could be forgiven, then you can also be forgiven for moral sin against your body, against another person, and against God.

Spiritual virginity is a real possibility, not a clever attempt to cover up sexual sin. For six years my wife and I worked with street kids and hippies. They had usually been sexually active for years. When they came to Christ and received forgiveness, you could actually see a glow of spiritual virginity on their faces.

I think that's what happened to Mary Magdalene. When she was forgiven by Jesus she received the glow of spiritual virginity. Her sinful activity was part of her past, but her spiritual virginity was restored as a gift from the Holy Spirit.

Every time I see that transformation repeated it is truly exciting. When I see a woman or man who has slept with all kinds of partners receive that glow, it is a beautiful experience. That's why I'm so eager to convince single moms who have been involved in an indiscretion that marriage is not the solution to the guilt they feel. Forgiveness from God and restoration by His Holy Spirit is the answer.

Are you ready to stay single and parent your children through to adulthood? Would you at least prayerfully consider the idea? I hope so, for I've seen too many devastated women who have been through the wringer a second time or struggle in a tense, blended family. The alternatives to remaining single often are filled with more difficulties.

SUMMARY

Are you considering, or currently involved in, another relationship? Here's my advice:

Set your moral limits before you start a relationship. Set the physical limit at 7 or less, according to the scale on page 117.

Don't steal energy from your kids to invest in a relationship.

Commit your life to spiritual virginity.

Give yourself time to heal—*all* the time you need to regain emotional, physical, mental, and spiritual equilibrium. That's the only way to true recovery.

TEN

The Weekend War

If you're like most single parents, you've gone through the weekend exchange of children several times . . . maybe dozens of times. What's been your experience? Lots of encouragement and smiles all around?

Probably not! For many single parents, child custody is simply all-out war. That's why I call it the Weekend War, and you and your ex the Weekend Warriors.

The weapons in this war? In some cases, the situation degenerates so far that the weapons are those of real warfare. Prior to that, however, the children are the weapons, and the trigger is pulled when the custody exchange takes place.

To build on this analogy, visitation can be viewed as a minefield. Both single parents plant land mines, hoping the other will step on one of them.

"When do I pick them up?"

"Where do I get them?"

"Why did you give this stuff to them?"

"Why did you give me a sick kid?"

These land mines are laid whenever you go back and

forth across that no man's land of exchanging children every other weekend and three months in the summer. And when someone steps on a mine, there may be not only verbal fireworks, but also broken doors and bruised bodies. The smoke of raging verbal abuse may linger in the nostrils for weeks.

REVENGE—THE DRIVING FORCE

Why do you and your ex do this to each other? Just a few years ago you were rational people who could at least be civil to each other much of the time. You even said "I do" in a civil ceremony. You may have been active in your church teaching a Sunday school class. Your ex may have been a deacon or an elder. And now, there for your children to see and experience, you're both acting like two preschoolers fighting over a toy in the sandbox.

I'm convinced that *revenge is the number one driving force in the Weekend War*. Your ex has hurt you so intensely that your moral restraints have been wiped out. There is no consideration of love and forgiveness, even though you know that's what the Bible is all about. The emotional pain is so intense it has covered up your faith. All you want to do is *punish, punish, punish*.

Why does rational reason go out the window? Is this a spiritual issue that a session with your pastor can change? Is it a physical issue because you're so worn out? Is it the emotional burnout you are experiencing?

Look back again at the diagram of the circle of energy in chapter 2 (see figure 3 on pages 28-29). At this stage of alienation, you probably have only 5 percent of your mental energy, 5 percent physical, and 5 percent spiritual; your emotional rage is consuming the other 85 percent of your energy. I tell single parents that they're largely missing the energy resources containing rational thought processes and controls.

Now I know this may sound odd, but I see it constantly in singles. All they have is emotional energy, and that energy is so overpowered with rage and hate that *there is no rational reality*. Their actions become unexplainable from the perspective of logic—except the logic of rage and revenge (see figure 2, "Steps of Destruction," on page 24).

When two people with this level of rage come together for a weekend exchange of children, the result can be a massive flash of lightning and the powerful reverberations of thunderclaps. And standing there, illuminated by the lightning and almost deafened by the thunder, are your children. Every week they go through it, hoping against hope that mom and dad will work things out soon.

NO WINNERS—JUST PRISONERS

There are no winners in this war. Both you and your ex are trying to get back at each other, and the wounds caused by the conflict only intensify the separation and reduce the potential for any form of reconciliation. Your children receive wounds that, without spiritual maturity and professional counseling, may not heal for life. You are all taken prisoner by the tremendous forces at work.

Do you recall the story—covered in the national media—of Charles Rothenberg, the New Yorker who took his son, David, across country to Anaheim, California, without telling his ex? He knew she would not let him do it, so he did it secretly because he wanted to make points with his son and get back at his ex. Except that it rained on his parade, and for a week they had to stay in a motel instead of visiting Disneyland.

Then he called his ex. Almost crazy with fear by

this time, she heard Charles say that he and her son were in California. Not realizing her actions would push Charles over the edge both emotionally and rationally, she exploded in anger and screamed that he would never see his son again once she got him back.

What happens when a single parent does that to her ex? His mental energy probably was at zero because of the cross-country trip, the frustration of not being able to be a hero to his son, and the knowledge that his ex would be very angry.

Imprisoned by his own rage response, Rothenberg's reaction was tragic. He developed a plan for ultimate revenge—murder/suicide. Many an ex has planned a similar act in great detail but never carried it out. Charles partially succeeded. He poured gasoline over his son, lit it, and ran. But he did not have the emotional and mental energy left to carry out the suicide. Yet he did the most damaging thing he could do to his ex: he crippled and disfigured "her" son for life.

WHY YOU SHOULD CALL A
UNILATERAL CEASE-FIRE

Your situation may not have deteriorated anywhere near the Rothenburg tragedy, but it's likely that you may be exchanging hostilities or drawing battle lines. I want to convince you to call a unilateral—that is, one-sided—cease-fire.

Why should you bother trying to put a halt to the Weekend War? For the moment, forget the emotional damage of the fireworks, which is reason enough on its own. Let's get back to basics. Proverbs tells us, "A gentle answer turns away wrath" (15:1). A divorced husband who is treated kindly is more likely to write a check for child-support. Translation: *bread on the table, clothes to wear, money for recreation.*

"But isn't he *legally obligated* to provide child-support no matter what?" you ask. True; but the bitter reality is that only 44 percent of all fathers pay full child-support. And you could well be among the 56 percent who get only some or none of the support.

A research project by one of my interns, Don West, evaluated why fathers pay child-support and continue to visit their children. Common wisdom would say that the more money the father makes, the more he will pay in child-support. That the better he gets along with his kids, the more faithful he will be in child-support. Common wisdom is wrong on both counts.

Don's research showed that *the only constant determining the regularity of child-support was how well the ex-husband got along with his former spouse.* If he was making a million and did not get along with his ex-wife, forget the child-support. Even if he got along famously with his kids, it did not mean he would fulfill his legal obligation.

I know that what I'm going to say now may be too painful even to think about. But fiction—wrong ideas about child-support—won't change fact. *If you want child-support on a regular basis, be friendly to your ex.*

Let me put it another way: *Protect the relationship with your ex-husband.* Forget the fireworks, the "Why did you?" accusations. Be friendly to him and you will have a good chance of receiving money—enough money to keep the family going. Take some good advice from an impeccable source of wisdom, the Bible: "If possible, so far as it depends on you, be at peace with all men" (Romans 12:18). *Ouch.* From God's perspective, ex-husbands are as much in need of your peace as anyone.

And, taking it another step, what do we read earlier

in this chapter in the Bible? "Never pay back evil for evil to anyone" (verse 17). *Ouch again.*

RULES OF CONDUCT

Every mother connects visitation with child-support. And every father wants to see his child whether he pays or not. The man hooks his rights to visitation, while the woman hooks her rights to child-support. The war begins again! "But I thought that when the divorce was final I would have him *out* of my life forever!" Not so.

You can reduce hostilities in the Weekend War by observing a few simple Rules of Conduct for visitation.

Be Flexible
If Doug brings the check ten minutes late his ex will go back to court. Right off the bat. It's "take that for being late," with no understanding that he may have been held up in traffic, delayed in making a deposit, whatever.

Some time ago I worked with a separated couple who were coming to blows over a very simple issue. The ex-husband got paid every other Friday. The ex-wife however, went to court and had the judge set up child-support for the first and the fifteenth. Guess what? This arrangement didn't work out very well!

The two of them ended up fighting in my office. Finally, I said to them, "You guys have to solve this."

I proposed this to the woman: "I want you to go back to court and change the due date on your child-support to every other Friday." Turning to him I said, "And if you miss a payment, I want you to pay an extra half a month." Both of them felt this arrangement would work.

After four months of yelling at each other, the solution was as simple as that. But someone not involved emotionally had to bring objectivity (and a minor amount of creativity) into the situation. Their marriage had fallen apart because they had never learned conflict-resolution skills, so they didn't have any to resolve even this minor an issue. The fact is, they had developed conflict-generating skills, like most couples who divorce.

Be flexible. You'll find it goes a long way to bring peace.

Reverse the Roles

When all else fails, I resort to an old trick your parents probably pulled on you. I reverse the roles. I remember one day I brought my kids a candy bar. I gave it to one of my kids and said, "Divide it in half." I left the room and heard the crunch of the knife as it cut through the bar. Once the two pieces had been distributed I said, "Now trade."

You ought to have heard the scream. "I . . . I . . . I . . ." Who is the one screaming? That's right, the one who cut the candy bar.

As a single parent cries in my office about the Weekend War, I sometimes say, "Okay, imagine that your ex-husband has total custody of the children, and you want to visit them. How do you want to be treated?"

"That isn't fair," the woman may say. "You can't look at it that way. He always gets what he wants, and I don't want him to have that advantage any more."

"No," I say. "Let's turn the roles around. Let's give him 100 percent of custody. How do you want to be treated?"

"Well, I would want the children on my birthday."

"Then give him the children on his birthday," I say.

"But that isn't on his weekend."

"That's not the issue," I respond. "The issue is that

you need to treat him just like you would want to be treated. It hurts, but it's God's idea. And it works."

Seek Creative Alternatives

You may be saying, "But my ex won't even consider being nice to me. He seems to enjoy the Weekend War."

Maybe a creative alternative to meeting at your house or his apartment will take the fireworks out of the child exchange. Think for a moment about the range wars in the movies, between sheepherders and cattlemen. Or the gang wars for turf in today's big cities. Now think of your house as your turf. If your ex has to come there to pick up the children, he is emotionally at a disadvantage because he's on your turf. Same thing if you pick up the kids at his place. The logistics alone make the situation ripe for conflict.

One couple I know meets on the steps of the police department in their city. This is neutral turf that is very structured. Both parties seem to exhibit the best of behavior. Maybe you could drop the kids off at your folks, and your ex could pick them up there. Many counties have drop-in centers for kids, and you could do the exchange there.

Sometimes couples use the front office of our church because this is, with the exception of the police station, the only other place some people won't fight. Others meet in a restaurant where, if they act up, they embarrass themselves. Once they get far enough along in recovery, I suggest they go to a park, where they can both sit and watch their kids and not have to deal with each other.

DON'T LET THE WAR DRAG ON

What is the worst thing that can happen if you let the Weekend War drag on? Consider the "Steps of Destruction" chart (figure 2 on page 24), which shows the deterioration of a marriage from friendship to anger, then bitterness, next pugnaciousness, and finally death (suicide or murder). I show this chart to single parents as shock therapy if I can't get their attention any other way.

Weekend Wars can degenerate into pugnaciousness and physical violence. Sometimes it is the ex-husband breaking down the door of his ex-wife's house and physically attacking her. This happens more frequently than you might think. In some of these cases, the ex-husband eventually kills his ex-wife, or vice versa.

Both you and your ex must desire to stop the degeneration of the relationship if violence and even death are to be avoided.

SUMMARY

If your Weekend War is still complete with verbal fireworks, stop to think how you can develop a cease-fire. Remember God's Word, "A soft answer turns away wrath" (Proverbs 15:1). Follow these suggestions:

Focus on forgiveness and soft answers.

Don't go down the steps of destruction.

Treat your mate the way you want to be treated.

Begin the peace effort with a creative alternative, like meeting in a neutral place. Ask the Holy Spirit to help you go beyond that to genuinely forgive your ex and get on with life without the anger, hate, and bitterness which can destroy the two of you as well as your children. Start today to set the prisoners free. You'll find that you're truly on the road to recovery.

ELEVEN

The "R" Word Can Be the Key to Recovery

W e human beings are really quite amazing. We can love someone passionately for fifteen years, have many exciting adventures together, begin raising a family—and then the minute that person walks out on us we're overcome by bitterness, hatred, and thoughts of revenge. It's as though those experiences, those exciting adventures and good times, never happened.

Now that he's left you, he's suddenly become a sub-human enemy.

"Hold it!" you say. "The jerk didn't just leave. There was a history of abuse and of demeaning behavior. He doesn't even merit consideration as a human being."

Yes, there's often a valid basis for that kind of reaction. In fact, you may be responding, "Not only did he leave a trail of abuse, broken promises, and demeaning behavior, but he ran off with my best friend. I'm so angry I could kill him, her, or maybe both of them."

These feelings come naturally to fallen, sinful people. That's how we instinctively react to mistreatment. And that is usually the only level at which we will respond if we walk in the flesh and not in the Spirit.

I can almost hear you yell, "Don't get spiritual on me! If anyone's walking in the flesh it's my ex—*he's* the one you should be addressing."

Maybe. But since you're the one reading this book, not your ex, indulge me while I introduce an idea to you: a key step that could make an incredibly positive difference in your life.

RECONCILIATION IS NOT A FOUR-LETTER WORD

You may have guessed it—I'm talking about the "R" word: *reconciliation*. Though it may not be the kind of reconciliation you're thinking about.

I'm talking about reaching the point of being civil with your ex. Is reconciliation a bad word in your vocabulary? Then start with the first step: to give your ex the right to exist. On the following list, check as many rights as you're able to grant your ex right now.

- ❑ 1. No right to exist in the universe.
- ❑ 2. Right to exist in hell.
- ❑ 3. Right to exist on earth—in prison.
- ❑ 4. Right to exist on earth—free in Antarctica.
- ❑ 5. Right to exist on earth—in Africa.
- ❑ 6. Right to exist on same continent—North America.
- ❑ 7. Right to exist in same country.
- ❑ 8. Right to exist in same state.
- ❑ 9. Right to exist in same town.
- ❑ 10. Right to exist in same church.
- ❑ 11. Right to exist in same class.
- ❑ 12. Right to exist in chair next to me.
- ❑ 13. Right to speak to me when I wish.
- ❑ 14. Right to speak at will to each other.

❑ 15. Right to ride in the same car.
❑ 16. Right to be friends.
❑ 17. Right to go on a date with each other.
❑ 18. Right to restart our relationship.
❑ 19. Right to a deepen our new relationship.
❑ 20. Right to remarry each other.

Do you think that reconciliation could ever happen for you and your ex? It certainly has worked for many other single parents. Let's define it in simple terms: *When you can be in a public place with your former spouse without experiencing a surge of emotion or sudden rise in blood pressure, then you've reconciled with your ex.* Otherwise you're still working on it.

Still unsure why you should bother to consider reconciling with your ex? Let's examine a foundational biblical principle that may never have occurred to you, but that has truly long-range implications:

Therefore if any man is in Christ, he is a new creature; the old things passed away; behold, new things have come. Now all these things are from God, who reconciled us to Himself through Christ, and gave us the ministry of reconciliation, namely, that God was in Christ reconciling the world to Himself, not counting their trespasses against them, and He has committed to us the word of reconciliation.

Therefore, we are ambassadors for Christ, as though God were entreating through us; we beg you on behalf of Christ, be reconciled to God. He made Him who knew no sin to be sin on our behalf, that we might become the righteousness of God in Him. (2 Corinthians 5:17-21)

A proper understanding of this principle could dramatically affect your attitude toward reconciliation, and certainly toward remarriage.

WHAT'S IN A VOW?

Have you ever considered the implications of the vow you made when you married? If you're like most of us from the Baby Boomer generation, you probably haven't. We still don't like the word *commitment*. The problem is that God does consider commitment, and taking a vow—even a marriage vow—seriously.

Please understand that I'm not going in the back door to get you to consider remarrying your ex. I recognize that the relationship is now ruptured, and it would probably take a lot more than a discussion like this to change it. But the vow you took at the marriage altar has all kinds of implications beyond that issue.

Consider what God told Israel about making a vow: "When you make a vow to the LORD your God, you shall not delay to pay it, for it would be sin in you, and the LORD your God will surely require it of you" (Deuteronomy 23:21). He reinforces this in verse 23: "You shall be careful to perform what goes out from your lips, just as you have voluntarily vowed to the LORD your God, what you have promised." The next chapter in Deuteronomy, which discusses divorce and remarriage, makes it clear that these verses apply to the marriage relationship: specifically, to the wedding vow.

Or consider this passage, in which God lays down the law on vows relating to marriage: "If a man makes a vow to the LORD, or takes an oath to bind himself with a binding obligation, he shall not violate his word; he shall do according to all that proceeds out of his mouth"

(Numbers 30:2). In the next verse God turns to the woman: "Also if a woman makes a vow to the LORD, and binds herself by an obligation in her father's house in her youth, and her father hears her vow and her obligation by which she has bound herself, and her father says nothing to her, then all her vows shall stand." In those days the vows were made well in advance of the wedding day.

What happens if that woman or man gets divorced? Read on to verse 9: "But the vow of a widow or of a divorced woman, everything by which she has bound herself shall stand against her."

Ouch. That's a tough stance indeed. Yet that's how seriously God looks at vows—the commitments we make to each other. The issue of reconciliation must be viewed from the context of the vows we make and how well we keep them.

So even though divorce has separated you from your ex, in God's eyes the commitment to love him has not been wiped out. It can, in fact, become the foundation for those first few tentative steps toward reconciliation. And it seems to me it should also be a key consideration when another man wants to take you to the marriage altar. In a day of "easy come, easy go" disposable relationships, we especially ought to let God's Word serve as our guide.

Okay, now that I've laid the heavy one on you, are there other reasons for reconciliation, at least to the point of being civil to your ex? You bet there are!

THE BENEFITS OF RECONCILIATION

Most single moms I know are looking for a man to be a father to their children. Of course they're also looking for someone to love and support them, but the driving intent is to provide a father for the children, especially the boys.

However, my experience is that assuming there's no history of abuse or other extremely harmful behavior, this parental need can most easily be met by reconciliation with the children's real father.

In many cases it takes much less effort and time to make the first relationship work than to get the second one to fly. Just think of the time and effort it took to get your first marriage off the ground. Think of how much emotional energy you burned up. Even though your ex is not living with you, you know his strengths and weaknesses. You know how firm or lax he will be in discipline, what the risk of abuse is, and how dependable he will or won't be.

Not so for any new man who comes into your life. We're living in an era of easy relationships and of the deadly AIDS virus (according to Josh McDowell, there are more than fifty-seven sexually transmitted diseases). There are con artists who make a career of living off women who are easy prey because of their strong desire for a new relationship. Weaving your way through this cultural maze to develop a friendship, seeing that through to a relationship, and finally building a marriage becomes an all-consuming, sometimes dangerous task.

It isn't much easier, and maybe harder, single moms tell me, to reconcile to the level of friendship with their ex. But there are side benefits, such as more consistent child-support and help when a crisis arises in your home.

At the same time you will need to come up to the friendship level anyway to release your heart before you can successfully go on to another relationship. Otherwise you'll drag all your emotional baggage, all your feelings of guilt and anger, into your next relationship and maybe doom it to failure.

Your resentment will bleed all over the other person in the new relationship, and you will continue to use up emotional energy harboring that bitterness and hostility. You desperately need this energy if the new relationship is to work. This lack of emotional energy is a key reason why most second marriages break up within seven years (60 percent, according to the Census Survey).

In addition to freeing up needed energy, reconciling to the point of friendship also permits single parents to come back to a point of stability. It tells them that they have achieved some level of SELF stability: Spiritually, Emotionally, Lovingly, and Financially.

That regained stability releases energy that you've been using to maintain your hostility to your ex. This energy is now available for the children and for yourself. You and your kids need all the energy you can muster to heal emotionally and manage as a single mom.

In an earlier chapter we focused on how child-support is affected by your relationship with your ex. There's just no getting around it: if you're able to reconcile to the level of friendship you will almost certainly guarantee more consistent child-support and smoother visitation arrangements.

STEPS TO RECONCILIATION

You may be at least half-convinced that you ought to be reconciled with your ex to the point of friendship. Yet that's easier said than done, isn't it? Let's walk through some steps you can take toward reconciliation.

As we do so, remember two things. First, just as love is an act of the will, so *initiating reconciliation is an act of the will.* Second, *reconciliation is a process,* and it will take time. A lot of time—maybe as much as five years.

Consider taking these steps toward reconciliation and recovery from your divorce:

1. *Become friendly toward your ex-husband.* Let go of the anger, bitterness, and hostility that is consuming you and draining your energy. This is partly an act of the will, but must be reinforced by the power of the Holy Spirit.

You can't take this step toward reconciliation without spiritual stabilization. This stabilization is regained over time as you attend church, pray, read the Bible, and become part of a support group. Only the Holy Spirit can give you the power to *act* right when you don't *feel* right.

But once you know what to do and then actually do it, you'll feel a lot better. This reinforces that God really is with you and that you can take the next step.

Part of the process of becoming friendly is recognizing that your ex is a person worthy of respect and God's love. A man once said to me, "After I started treating my wife with a little dignity and respect, it's amazing how much she changed." She was just reacting to his attitude up to that point. I've seen this happen over and over.

God wants us to forgive, absorb, deal with the anger—not camp out in it.

2. *Do special things for your ex-husband.* Feelings follow actions. Being friendly to your ex breaks the ice. Now you can begin to do special things for him that will restore your relationship to the friendship level.

In my daily planner I've noted the day my wife's sister died—and every year I transfer it to my new calender. No one else keeps track of that date except my wife and her parents. I try to acknowledge that day before it comes, for it's important to my wife: that was the day she lost her only sister. In fact, that was the day she lost her only sibling. If we were separated and wanted to reconcile, I would make sure I continued to remember that day.

Remember birthdays and anniversaries. Send a card or call. It can even take the sting out of having separated or having been served divorce papers on your birthday or anniversary—an all-too-frequent occurrence.

3. *Make a list of positives from the old relationship.* One way I help single parents regain objectivity is to have them write out a list of positives from the failed marriage. (They want to write down the negatives as well, so I tell them the list of negatives can never exceed the list of positives.)

If you're still living at the level of anger, bitterness, and pugnaciousness, you will have a long list of negatives and zero positives about your ex. But if you've moved back to the level of friendliness, you can actually begin a list of positives. In fact, doing this will help keep you from going back down again. Just writing the list out will help keep you in balance. Write that list now.

That list of positives ought to include more than the good qualities of your ex. It should recall the good things he did for you through the years, like keeping your car serviced, taking out the garbage, going with you to the doctor, taking you shopping, fixing things around the house, and visiting your parents. Beyond that, your list could include special events that you enjoyed, such as a special evening or a vacation that meant a lot to both of you.

IF YOU'RE STILL JUST SEPARATED

If you're only separated at this time there's another major benefit of reconciliation to the point of friendship. As one woman told me: "My husband and I worked out a do-it-yourself divorce. He was very generous with me and always paid his child-support." And they saved thousands of dollars in lawyers' fees.

I tell those who are separated that they might as well

divide their assets by four if they want to get a divorce the usual route. You get a fourth, he gets a fourth, and each of the attorneys gets a fourth. The harder the attorneys fight, the more they will receive, so sometimes they will actually generate conflict.

Your attorney may do it by insisting you demand 100 percent of the assets. Many a husband has come to me totally frustrated and angry. "She's asking for *everything*. Can you believe that?" he'll say.

I tell him, "Listen, your spouse didn't ask for that. Your spouse does not expect that. Her attorney is asking for that. You should have enough sense to know that no judge will leave you with nothing."

If you want to short-circuit that process, and save some assets for yourselves instead of giving them to your attorneys, then take steps toward reconciliation to the point of friendship with your ex. (A very helpful book in this area is *The Divorce Decision: The High Cost of Divorce.*[1])

"But my ex won't cooperate," you say. "He's not responding to any of my actions." That does happen occasionally, and you will have to accept that. If you've made friendly advances toward reconciliation, then what your ex does is his responsibility. In fact, sometimes you may need to wait six months, a year, or longer until he ends up disappointed in a current relationship. It's amazing how attractive you suddenly become.

Life is too short to live in anger, bitterness, and hostility. Your whole body needs the relief reconciliation can bring. Just imagine: you'll be able to walk into the same room with your ex and not even feel a knot in the stomach or the flushing of your face as your blood pressure rises. You'll actually be able to say hello to him, just like you do with other people.

SUMMARY

Remember these principles as you confront the "R" word:

To be successful in the future, you must deal with the past.

Commitments need to be kept.

Reconciliation is worth the time and money.

Reconciliation is possible because our Lord is the God of the impossible. The Holy Spirit who made you a new creation can also re-create in you feelings of friendliness, even agape or "other-centered" love, for your ex. Use the key of reconciliation to open the door to a new life of recovery.

TWELVE

Remarriage: Ready, Set . . . Wait a Minute!

B y now you know that I strongly support staying single until the children are grown. There are many reasons, but the central ones are that in light of AIDS and the current epidemic of child molestation, you and your children may be safer and better off without another relationship crowding your space. In addition, in most cases your children will do better with the focused attention of one parent, instead of the divided attention of two parents—one of them who may have little or no interest in being a father to your kids.

Somewhere along the way you will, however, develop more than a passing fancy for a man who's also looking for a lasting, intimate relationship. It may not happen until the children are grown—which would in many ways be wonderful—but it will probably happen sooner.

Before this happens, and certainly immediately after it happens, you ought to ask yourself a whole series of questions.

Now I know it may seem as though I'm putting up a barbed-wire fence between you and your dreams, but over the years I've seen scores of singles make both good and bad decisions. I've refined these questions accordingly, and I'm convinced they can help you make more good than bad decisions. So let's ask them for the sake of your and your kids' future happiness.

AM I FREE TO DATE?

What a ridiculous question, you may be thinking. *I'm an adult, I've been married once, and I'm not tied to the old taboos that once bound our parents.*

True, society says you're free to marry again. But what does the Bible have to say?

Jesus, His disciples, and the leadership of the early church took a tough position on divorce and remarriage. This biblical principle is laid out in Deuteronomy 24:4; Matthew 5:32, 19:9; and 1 Corinthians 7:10. From Jesus' perspective, only if your mate was involved in immorality, or your unbelieving spouse abandoned you, is a divorce permitted and by implication remarriage allowed.

Granted — you may not meet that biblical criteria, but you still want to remarry. What I'm giving you is the biblical standard. You need to make up your mind if you're willing to live by it.

AM I EMOTIONALLY FREE TO DATE?

Janet began to date three years after the divorce was final. She soon found that her heart had not healed from her last marriage. All the old wounds opened up again, and she had to pull out of the relationship. Janet had thought she was well until she tested her heart in this relationship.

One year later Janet entered into a friendship agreement with another man. A year after that they were married. This time, after five years, she was ready.

It's frequently been my experience that singles should not consummate that first relationship after divorce with marriage. It often seems that the first relationship helps the newly-divorced person get her bearings. Then she's ready for a longer-lasting second relationship, which can result in a successful marriage.

Developing a relationship with a person of the opposite sex is at best a tricky process. You're venturing into uncharted waters, many of which have hidden currents, rocks, even sharks lurking beneath the surface. Yet unless you're five years or more beyond the divorce date, your own emotional upheaval may distort your judgment.

Unfortunately, few single moms recognize how much emotional healing still needs to happen before they have the mental, spiritual, and physical energy to enter a new relationship. Here is a checklist that can help you determine if you are emotionally ready to date. Beware of a new relationship until you . . .

- can plan ahead for six months to a year;
- can read a book and develop notes from it;
- can balance your checkbook;
- have been reconciled to your ex to the point where you no longer get angry and can be civil to him when you're on the telephone or meet him in a public setting, or when your blood pressure does not go through the roof when you see him;
- have arrived at a level of contentment with singleness;
- are able to provide your children with loving emotional support when they experience their crises.

You may be thinking, "But I need the emotional support from a man to achieve that level of emotional strength." Not if you have been following through on the SELF process, achieving stability *spiritually* (with Jesus Christ at the center of your life and His Holy Spirit empowering you); *emotionally; lovingly* (through a support network); and *financially.*

Emotionally stressed-out persons make difficult life partners. They drain a marriage, rather than contributing through sincere love. That's why dating and marriage on the rebound from a divorce too often end up in disaster.

HAVE I STABILIZED MY LIFE?

The process of stabilizing your life is a full-time occupation. Your hands are full with taking care of yourself and your children. For most single moms the most pressing issues all relate to finances—finding housing you can afford, clothing the kids, educating yourself to find a better job, maintaining a car, finding the money to send the kids to camp.

During this time you will also be re-contacting the family, reestablishing the family support network, getting into a support group at church. These relationships, though not as complex because many of them existed previously, still take time and energy to stabilize.

Finally, you will be getting over your anger at God for letting you experience the divorce, and moving from asking "why?" to "what now?" With God in the picture, stability will happen a lot sooner.

Your level of stability will determine whether you will be a contributor or withdrawer in a future dating or marriage relationship. Until you become a contributor you will *not* attract the men who thrive in a healthy relationship. Instead, you will attract men who exhibit strong symptoms of codependency, resulting in another confusing and damaging relationship.

I describe this experience as two one-legged people hopping around looking for someone to hold them up. They find each other and think they have stability. Did you ever try to sit on a two-legged stool? Even if one partner is emotionally stable and has both feet on the ground, that person is going to feel like the total contributer while the other mate begins to make withdrawals from the relationship. We now have a three-legged stool that works fine, but one partner is a contributer and the other is a withdrawer. When the withdrawals exceed the contributions, the relationship or marriage fails.

ARE MY CHILDREN READY?

John was eight years old and really wanted a daddy. He would ask every man his mother brought around if he would be his daddy. His mother, Helen, was so overwhelmed by his desire that she married Jack to have a father for her son. It turned out that Jack contributed to the marriage while Helen made withdrawals.

After five years of living with his stepfather, John, now a teen, rebelled against his stepdad. Sadly, the marriage failed. Helen now found herself a single mom raising an angry son.

When you're hurting after a divorce, it's easy to make one of two mistakes. The first is to think only of your need of companionship, of someone to hold you and make you feel important again. You've been so beaten down during the events leading to separation and divorce that there's nothing showing on the self-esteem thermometer. A relationship can make you feel like an attractive woman again.

The second mistake is to think only of your children, especially if you have a son. Getting him a father is paramount in your thinking—and the sooner the better. Yet the distraction of a new relationship can actually diminish the attention and emotional support he will receive from you.

So don't rush into finding a new parent for your children, for the kids will all too soon be gone. You will face spending the rest of your life with a man who served as a parent but may be lacking what you need in a husband.

Children are a rich inheritance from God, so you need to give them full consideration before you date or remarry. Just like adults, kids also need time to heal from the trauma of a divorce. Just because they're not showing the emotional stress as obviously doesn't mean they're not experiencing it. Dad may still be an important memory—and if they're visiting with him regularly they may not want or need another parent.

If you marry again while the kids are young you may actually be significantly increasing their stress levels, and creating potentially explosive situations for yourself.

AM I JUST LOOKING FOR COMPANIONSHIP?

Single people tend to think of companionship as a by-product of marriage. If they get married they'll have it. Yet the number of divorces today demonstrates that companionship is not a given in marriage. If you're a single parent looking for companionship, there are other options to consider besides marriage.

One option may be your family, though today's mobility takes us away from the companionship provided by a mother or sister, or even a grandmother or aunt.

Another option, and probably a more viable source

of companionship, is with someone of the same sex. One of the reasons your marriage did not work may be that neither of you had an intimate same-sex friend before marriage, so now is the time to focus on that. You may find these same-sex friends at a divorce recovery group at church, at work, at Little League ballgames, at PTA meetings—wherever you meet other women with similar interests. Develop these skills with the same sex before you start again with the opposite.

CAN I AFFORD TO DATE?

For the single mom struggling to buy milk and pay the rent, the cost of a date may be too high. By the time you total up the extras—a new hairstyle, a new outfit—and baby-sitting expenses, a date may be as truly unaffordable as a new car.

You'll also find more emancipated men today who don't automatically grab for the check in a restaurant, for whom "going Dutch" has become a pattern. I'm constantly amazed how many single moms are actually paying most of the costs of a dating relationship.

AM I WILLING TO BE HURT AGAIN?

Remember those dating years in high school, and the times your heart was crushed by rejection? You've just come through a rejection so severe that its trauma may be greater than all of your high school rejections combined. Setting out on a new dating relationship could be another setup for the "blues." Can you emotionally survive another broken relationship?

Remember, you only have so much emotional energy—and you need to conserve that energy for the healing process and for taking care of your children. Don't fritter it away on another high-risk dating adventure. Later on when you have a surplus of emotional energy, it will be an entirely different situation.

WHAT DO MY FAMILY MEMBERS THINK?

Unless you were raised in an unusually dysfunctional family, your parents not only love you deeply but probably have a surprisingly good idea of what kind of person you are and what kind of person you should marry. Why not seek their help now?

Your parents have also seen you on both your good days (and years) and your bad days (and years). They can be amazingly perceptive of where you are emotionally, spiritually, financially. Let them be part of your accountability structure!

You've driven through those construction zones with the flagperson holding up the "Go Slow" sign. Wouldn't you rather obey the sign than wreck your car? Your parents may be able to flag you with a "Go Slow" sign that can keep you from another marriage disaster.

DO I HAVE CLEAR MORAL STANDARDS?

Some people think you shouldn't even have to ask this question if you are a born-again believer. But my twenty years with Christian singles has revealed how thin the veneer of Christianity can be in the area of morality. One of the reasons many marriages fail is that there was premarital sex. That lack of moral restraint can destroy a key ingredient of marriage — integrity. Moral integrity means you can be trusted not to sleep with someone you aren't married to.

A single mom is faced every day with modeling Christian behavior for her children. She really wants them to remain sexually pure as they approach marriage. So she must make up her mind to limit her physical involvement in dating to expressions of affection that are not sexually intimate.

Until you regain your emotional stability, *you don't have the mental and spiritual energy to say no when exposed to temptation.* You may have sound moral values, but under the stress of physical intimacy, they can evaporate like water on a hot griddle.

WILL MY DATING AFFECT RECONCILIATION?

Is this question of little interest to you? I need to remind you that your ex will quite likely recycle back to the line of reconciliation at least once, if not more often, during the first two years after the divorce. If you're in a dating relationship at that time, he will wander off and a great opportunity to achieve reconciliation will have been squandered.

I'm not necessarily talking about reconciliation for remarriage, but about the opportunity to establish reconciliation to the friendship level for the sake of you and your children. (The details of this process are covered in my book *Reconcilable Differences.*[1])

AM I EMOTIONALLY READY FOR ANOTHER DIVORCE?

As you think of a dating relationship you may be thinking of the joy it's going to bring you, and rightly so. But even though in our culture many date only for companionship reasons, I find that Christians are usually not comfortable with that. They date as a prelude to marriage.

Yet what did the first marriage bring you? Are you ready for a rerun of the frustration, the hurt in trying to make a marriage work, and maybe even the pain of divorce? If not, stick to other activities and raise the children God has left in your care.

WILL I BE ABLE TO MEET
ALL MY FINANCIAL OBLIGATIONS?

For most single moms, the fear of poverty is always at hand. *Things will be different this time,* you say to yourself, as you begin to date a good-looking professional man. Somehow he always has money when you need it during the dating period. But after the wedding it's another story—he's always behind on the bills. What happened? Here's a scenario that occurs more often than you might think.

Credit cards—he used them to give the appearance of wealth. What he didn't tell you about are his child-support payments to two former spouses. So now even your combined income doesn't make it, and you are devastated.

A second divorce will not be any cheaper than the first. That's why so many single moms stay poor—they keep spending their money on desperate attempts at happiness.

HAVE I FACED THE POSSIBILITY OF CHILD ABUSE?

In an earlier chapter we pointed out the high incidence of child abusers among Christian divorced single men. We have finally opened our eyes to this problem, but confidentiality laws have a way of jamming up the information pipeline. How many of us would even think to call a new flame's ex?

So you may never know until it happens that your new husband abuses children—not only emotionally and physically, but also sexually. Are you prepared for that? Of course, not every prospective partner is an abuser, but making background checks—for your well-being as well as your children's—doesn't hurt. (If you can't make a phone call or two, perhaps a friend can do it for you.)

HOW IMPORTANT IS MY CHURCH?

Which of these three were key contributors to your marriage failing: money, children, or religion? A surprising number of divorces occur when one of the spouses becomes a Christian, entering into a vital personal relationship with Jesus Christ. Others may happen when one spouse joins a cultic group.

So how important is your local church to you? Will your new husband share your loyalty?

Ray and Jean had been married only ten months when he wanted out. He came into her world and married her so that he could take her back into his world. When she chose to stay with the church and not go into his world, he left her. His interest in spiritual things had begun its decline the day after they started premarital counseling.

Even singles groups in large churches can be danger zones. Because many small churches don't have singles groups, men and women from various denominations gravitate to larger churches. Once a person remarries, his loyalty may gravitate back to the original church he came from. Being a Lutheran and marrying a Baptist may not seem such a big thing when you meet a man at the singles group, but two to five years later he may suddenly develop total loyalty to his denomination, which may bring you to a point of decision over theological issues.

WHAT IS THE AGE DIFFERENCE?

A significant difference in age may present problems you might not initially anticipate. In today's world a difference of ten years can put a man and a woman in different cultures. They may not even enjoy the same musical groups or admire the same movie stars. If he was a teen during the turbulent sixties and she was a teen during the low-key late seventies, many of their values and tastes may be different.

Each of us carries a certain amount of cultural baggage, so we must be aware of potential incompatibilities that a significant age difference might stir up. After working with hundreds of single mothers who remarried, I've found that if there is more than a five-year difference in age, people need to consider this issue carefully.

AM I READY FOR MORE CHILDREN?

Let's say you bring two children into the relationship, and he brings two. You both agree that four is enough of a roomful. Then you get married. I can almost guarantee it, one day one of you will say, "Wouldn't it be nice to have just one of our own?" The person who says no in that situation may win the argument but lose the war—the relationship may never be the same again. So are you ready for more children?

AM I PREPARED FOR A FIGHT
OVER INHERITANCE?

Why would I bring up inheritance when you have thirty to fifty years before it even becomes an issue? Unfortunately, I've seen some awful struggles over inheritances in blended or compounded families. Money, valuable household items, property, all suddenly take on new significance at the time of a partner's death. And the bad blood that results tests the depth of our Christianity.

Now I know this one issue will not prevent you from going out on a date. But when it's considered in light of all the other questions, it gains significance. There are less painful ways to live and die than married, divorced, remarried, divorced, and remarried again . . . and then cap it off with a bitter fight over the inheritance.

THINK TWICE

Ever walk through a dark room in your house and keep bumping into furniture? Wouldn't it be nice if someone had put even a spot of reflective tape on the various pieces of furniture? How much pain could that have saved?

The questions I've raised in this chapter are like pieces of reflective tape: They're designed to reduce the number of bumps and bruises you experience as a single mom. A broken toe is no fun . . . neither is a broken second marriage.

SUMMARY

Don't leave this chapter without keeping these thoughts in mind:

Be sure before God that you are free to marry —
before you date.

Think twice before marrying the first man who kisses you
after the separation.

Refuse to live on a two-legged stool.

There are good reasons for staying single until your kids are grown. If you're contemplating remarriage, whether now or later, stop to consider the issues I've raised before you head into such a major commitment. And if you need more incentives for staying single, read the next chapter on what happens when you start mixing families together. It's not an easy recipe. You may find yourself saying, *ready, set — wait a minute!*

THIRTEEN

Blended and Compounded Families

L et's say a single father of two and a single mother of three decide to marry and create a new household with all of them under the same roof. What can we say about what's going to happen in this new web of family dynamics?

Not a whole lot, really. Despite a number of books by people in blended families, we can't predict what will actually go on when a single mom and a single dad, each with children, get married. The possibilities are too numerous and complex. The best we can do is understand the existing factors that will shape those possibilities.

In order to examine the variety of relationships created when two existing families are joined, first we need to clarify definitions. I distinguish between a *blended family*—the marriage of a single mother with children and a single male with no experience with children; and a *compounded family*—the marriage of two single parents, each with children. The different factors present in these situations create very different dynamics.

THE BLENDED FAMILY

Let's first consider the blended family and the relationship problems that arise when a single mom with children weds a never-married man. Which combination is the most likely to succeed, and which has the potential to create the most severe problems?

The worst-case scenario, in my opinion, is when a single mom with only a son enters into marriage with a single, never-married, and childless guy. This combination is like putting a blasting cap into a keg of dynamite and lighting the fuse. It's only a matter of time before the dynamite explodes. What tends to happen in this type of marriage?

The single guy comes into the marriage expecting to be head of the house: in effect, to establish the authority structure. His new wife may have told him that she wants him to be the spiritual leader as well. Yet the new husband walks into a home with a preexisting authority structure that has most likely been functioning for a number of years if the boy is six years old or over. Mom and son have developed a dynamic that works—he knows when he needs to obey immediately and when he can dawdle. He knows his mother's moods, recognizing when it's not good to cross her.

After the beautiful wedding and honeymoon night, the man walks into the home and installs himself as head of the house. What a great feeling—he's finally a husband and father. Within the first four to five hours of the first day he probably will ask the boy to get something or to clean up some scattered toys.

What does the boy do? He remembers his chain of command, so before he does anything he looks to his mother, checking with her either visually or verbally.

The mother sees it as a natural response, since she has not yet emotionally adapted to her new husband as head of the house.

But the new father invariably sees this as an act of rebellion, so he sets out to establish his authority in the home. First he tries to do it verbally. In almost all cases the son then heads for his mother and says, in one way or another, "I don't have to do what he says, do I Mom? Please?" The new father's instinctive reaction? He lays hands on the boy. Flesh to flesh.

As soon as the man touches the boy it's as if he has walked between a mama grizzly bear and her cub. Wham! The mother blindsides her new husband, sometimes physically attacking him. He did not expect this, since he thought she would support his effort to bring her son under control.

How does the new husband and father react? Instinctively, he defends himself and strikes back verbally or physically at his new wife. Before he realizes it the boy has now become the aggressor as well, attacking his new father with whatever is at hand. It's two against one, odd man out!

Guess how long the new father sticks around? In most of these cases the man leaves, driven out of the house by the intensity of this first attempt at discipline. And just as often he never returns; a divorce comes next, and the family is back to mother and son.

Part of the problem is that the man really doesn't understand kids. He vaguely remembers that children are supposed to sit and be quiet, and if they don't they need to be brought into line. The new husband usually has no clue regarding the impact of his trying to establish a new authority structure in a home that already has one smoothly functioning.

Louise, a single mom with a ten-year-old son, married Roy, a single man who had spent many of his growing-up years in a foster home and was finally adopted. Roy was determined to start the relationship right, so he started spending time with Louise's son well before the wedding date. They developed a good friendship.

To Roy's chagrin, he discovered that once the wedding bells had rung, the son no longer considered him a friend. Now Roy was an authority figure. When the boy failed to respond to his verbal directions, Roy attempted corporal punishment. The mother intervened and a stand-off resulted: Louise and her son against Roy.

Within a few days the whole marriage relationship was in jeopardy. A temporary solution was for the boy to go and stay with his father. But this triggered another struggle: Louise now had to deal with resentment over the loss of her son. After several months of counseling, reconciliation was effected, with the son returning home again under an agreement whereby only Louise would administer corporal punishment. This might have been a poor working arrangement, but it was better than none.

Louise is now expecting another child. But in my opinion, she and Roy will not go through the same problems because they will be raising their own child, not Louise's.

A less volatile relationship results from the marriage of a never-married man to a mother with one or more daughters. It's less volatile because the man doesn't feel he has to exercise control over a daughter as he does a son, so he'll let the mother intervene and handle the rebellion.

Normally the new husband will not put up with bad-mouthing and similar outright rebellion, but he will appeal to the mother and get her support. Then the two will try to work at smoothing out the relationship with the daughter—something that seldom happens as easily with a son.

Also, blending a family by adding a never-married woman to a single-father family is easier because the authority structure is already established.

THE COMPOUNDED FAMILY

Robert and Brenda met in the singles group at our church. She had full custody of her three children, and he had weekend visitation rights for his four children. After many months of dating and premarital counseling, they were married, with the full understanding that they might end up with all the children.

Robert's former wife became ill during the first year of his marriage to Brenda, and his four children landed back in his lap. Brenda and Robert now had seven children in a small, three-bedroom house.

Today, eight years later, Robert and Brenda are still married. All but two of the children are gone from home, but there have been many conflicts and many tears. The moral of the story is that it's wise to count the cost (and the children!) before blending or compounding a family.

On the positive side, authority relationships are more easily established in compounded families. This is because the compounded family brings together a single mom with children and a single dad with children. Both spouses have experience with children. And the father brings an established authority structure with him through the relationship he has established with his children. At least his children usually accept his authority in the home and do what he asks them to do.

The mother also finds it much easier to accept his authority if he brings children into the marriage. He automatically has some credibility as a parent and is accepted for having some knowledge of how children respond. That is, unless he tries something stupid, like forcing the kids to do something that kids just don't do.

I remember a stepfather who had grown up in a penny-pinching home, where each child was allotted only two pieces of toilet paper per event. He tried to impose this limitation on his stepchildren—and the mother came unglued!

If a stepfather brings boys and the stepmother brings girls into the compounded family, the new family has the best chance of surviving. He will have established his authority over the sons, which is critical, and she and he together can manage the girls. If, on the other hand, she has boys and he has girls, there is a greater danger of fireworks. He is again trying to exercise authority over a "man," and he will still get the reaction I described earlier, though the violence level is typically much lower because he has some developed parenting skills.

MULTIPLIED RELATIONSHIPS

I've been describing the most basic relationships in a blended or compounded family—those within each family group. Yet beyond that small circle of relationships lurk the hidden dangers of multiplied relationships, each of which eats up emotional energy, generates astonishing levels of trauma, and sometimes even breaks up marriages. And these relational complexities particularly affect children.

There are a number of ways to look at and visualize the expansion of relational possibilities. For some people I counsel it has been helpful to introduce a mathematical formula that projects these possibilities.

Others who are more visually oriented find it helpful to draw a chart with stick figures to view how many people are involved, with a line connecting each figure to the other.

The mathematical formula I use may make sense to you (though it comes out of my engineering background, it's valid in evaluating the complexity of relationships). On the other hand, you may want to take a piece of paper and draw stick figures representing the people involved as I explain them.

Here's the formula: The total number of possible relationships at any given point in time equals the square of the number of people involved, minus the number of people involved, leaving a sum that is then divided by two.

Confused? Look at this mathematical formula:

Figure 5
Formula for the total number of interpersonal relationships possible

P = Total number of people

I = Total number of possible interpersonal relationships

$$I = \frac{(P \times P) - P}{2}$$

In this formula, "I" equals the total number of relationships possible, while "P" equals the number of people involved.

Let's look at how this relationship factor begins simply enough and then gets incredibly complex as families break up and parents remarry. Consider what happens when Jack marries Jill for the first time. Add mother and father on both sides, and you have six people involved (leaving out brothers and sisters right now, just to simplify the example).

Now let's work the formula: "P" = 6, so 6 times 6, or 36, minus 6, leaves 30. Now divide the 30 by 2, and you get 15 different relational possibilities.

Out of those 15 possibilities, which is typically the most volatile? Right: the one between Jack's mother and Jill, since both are emotionally involved with the same man, and often are trying to control the same man.

Which is the next most volatile? Jack's relationship with Jill's mother, since the mother has a vested interest in the success or failure of her daughter. If she has also been used to controlling her daughter for many years, she now faces handing over control to an interloper—her son-in-law.

Jack and Jill get a divorce before they have any children. What happens with the number of possible relationships? Let's say Jack and Jill both remarry, and in each new marriage there are 6 relationships. Since the divorce does not always break the relationships developed during that first marriage, we now have 12 people involved instead of 6 (2 more spouses and 4 more parents).

Let's run the formula again and see what happens: "P" = 12, so 12 times 12, or 144, minus 12, leaves 132. Now divide the 132 by 2, and you get 66 possible interpersonal relationships—which all need to work reasonably smoothly for the new couples to be happy. Life *can* get very complicated. And this is without factoring in children!

Let's suppose that John and Jane each bring 2 children into their marriage to form a compounded family. Add the 4 children to the adults involved (John, Jane, their parents, their ex-spouses, and their ex-spouses' parents) and you get 16 people for the "P" quantity. "P" squared, or 16 times 16, is 256. Subtract 16 from that number and you get 240, which when divided by 2 leaves 120 possible relationships. I guarantee you that there is no chance of total harmony when there are that many possible relationships. Life now *is* very complicated!

Happiness and contentment relate directly to the complexity of your life. As any management model reveals, the simpler things are, the easier they are to handle. Single-parent families are difficult; blended families are very complex; and compounded families offer the potential for tremendous stress and ultimate breakdown.

The fact is that we have great difficulty achieving happiness with 15 in our relationship circle. Life gets miserable at 66 relationships, and totally unbearable at 120. We can't juggle that many relationships successfully.

WHAT HAPPENS TO THE CHILDREN

What happens to children when they end up with more than fifteen possible relationships?

Generally, at first children like all the stimulation. When Robert and Brenda married, for example, with her three and his four, the children initially loved the excitement and the family pulled together to make peace and keep it all together. When the conflicts of complexity began, the parents both quit trying to solve all of the conflicts and focused just on the critical ones. The children responded by gravitating toward a few selected relationships.

For some young boys this relationship might be a special grandfather, who is now an ex-grandfather. This interaction produces a strain for the new marriage because it constantly introduces the ex-father-in-law back into this new marriage. This also involves the boy's natural father, and the excitement begins. "I want to go live with my dad!" is the battle cry.

Interestingly, sometimes the interpersonal relationships with pets are stronger than they are with humans.

When families are brought together there may be a favorite pet that becomes part of "mine," "yours," and "ours." A child may use the pet as an escape from having to deal with all the complex new relational patterns he or she is being exposed to.

SUMMARY

So think before you leap into a relationship with a man who promises to meet all your needs. He brings a whole web of relationships with him that have no relevance to you until you're married. After the wedding these relationships can entrap you and spoil your happiness with the new love of your life.

If you want to heal personally and provide your children with the kind of loving attention they so desperately need, remaining single may be your best option. Obviously, some remarried families succeed, but they are not the norm.

Use these thoughts to check yourself before jumping into a new family structure:

Marrying a never-married man without kids creates the most difficult situation.

If you had followed your parents' advice, would you have married your last spouse?

Remind yourself of the formula for projecting the number of interpersonal relationships created through remarriage.

Is there really a way to measure if you're a successful single parent? In the next chapter we'll look at some benchmarks that help show what successful single parenting is all about.

FOURTEEN

Am I Succeeding as a Single Parent?

Y ou're ready to put some of the principles in this book into practice. But you're wondering how you'll know if you're being successful as a single mom.

Is success having a steady, responsible job like Susan, who also continues to be active in her church? Her two daughters are in their early twenties and doing well. Susan is really proud of how they turned out, even though their father hasn't been involved with them in years.

Or maybe success resembles Josie's story. She tried suicide after divorce and failed. Then she called a friend who asked her if she had a personal relationship with God. Josie didn't know you could have that kind of relationship with God, but one day she asked God to help her. He surprised her with His presence.

Fourteen years later, Josie is a vivacious, enthusiastic Christian who speaks at women's clubs and retreats. Her oldest daughter was a straight A student in high school; won many awards in sports, including athlete of the year; was selected homecoming queen; and shows remarkable spiritual maturity. The second daughter has struggled much more, especially in view of the shadow her sister cast. Would you be happy with that scenario?

For every single-parent family that turns out like Susan's I can name many more who have struggled, had rebellious kids, saw a son or daughter move in with the father and repudiate the mother's faith. Yet should we label them unsuccessful?

PERSONAL BENCHMARKS

"Hold it!" you might be saying. "You're way ahead of me. I'm only two years into single parenting, and I need something or someone to tell me that I'm doing okay, that I'm succeeding at least on some level. I need some benchmarks or checkpoints that can reassure me along the way."

I'm going to list a number of questions you can ask yourself to guide you in evaluating your progress through recovery. These are broad, general indicators, but I believe they can be very helpful in identifying the kinds of issues that influence your success as a single mom.

(As you read through the following benchmarks, think back to the energy circles in figure 3, pages 28-29. You might want to go back and take a look at them once again to refresh your memory.)

How Much Emotional Energy Am I Still Burning Up?
This is the first question to ask yourself. Just after your divorce, your emotional energy needs were so high that you were left with perhaps just 15 percent of your total energy. Small wonder you couldn't run a marathon (or around the block), make strawberry jam in the evening after a day at the office, lead a Bible study, or coach your son's softball team.

You're succeeding in this area if you're burning up less

than 50 percent of your energy on emotions. You can sense this when you perceive a lifting of the weight off your life. You feel you might even have a little breathing room.

How Am I Responding Emotionally to the Opposite Sex?

When you're still hurting badly from the divorce proceedings, you don't have energy to focus on the opposite sex. Once you're making good progress in your recovery, however, you're coming alive. When a member of the opposite sex looks at you, he no longer sees a woman oozing emotional hurt. You become intriguing, and that person will begin to focus emotional energy on you.

What a tremendous change! Instead of your losing energy to other people, someone is giving energy to you.

As a counselor I'm one of the first to know when that happens. A single mom will come to me and say, "This man approached me and said, 'Hi.' I don't know what to do!" She may not be ready to handle his attention yet, but the guy has seen something and is interested.

The next stage is when a single mom comes to me and says, "I saw this guy in singles, and felt something stirring for the first time in years. I really felt attracted to him. That hasn't happened to me in a long time!" That's another checkmark along the way indicating that you're recovering emotionally.

How Much Personal Energy Is Returning?

Once you start regaining mental energy you will find you can concentrate longer. Reading an entire book will no longer be such a chore. Your Bible reading will be easier and you will comprehend more.

Another sign of increasing personal energy, mentally and physically, is when you can comfortably handle your own finances. You find youself saving money for something special because you're making wiser purchases and you're keeping your budget under control.

These benchmarks indicate that you're able to focus enough to plan for more than a few hours ahead. Now you're making appointments not just for next week, but for next month. Next summer's vacation is scheduled. That's progress, real progress! You now have the mental energy to look into the future.

Sometimes I ask a single mom, "What are you doing for a hobby?"

"I don't have a hobby," she'll say. "I just chase kids."

She's right, for her energy is all gone. What may take me twenty minutes to do, can take her an hour. When she completes the task she is physically exhausted.

Yet hobbies are a crucial measurement of stability. They require the ability to finish your work in a timely manner and schedule time and money as necessary.

BENCHMARKS IN YOUR PARENTING

What are some of the things you want to achieve with your child or children? Do you have some specific ideas, or—like so many parents—are you just hoping for the best as you live day by day?

If you want to measure your progress as a single mom, you need to establish some goals. Here are several questions worth considering as benchmarks for your parenting.

Am I Leading My Child into Loving Relationships?
Too few parents are teaching their children *what* love is, *how* to love, *whom* to love, and *what kind* of love they need to have and give. We need to lead them into relationships where they will understand that it's all right to hug or kiss

someone: boys, for example, should be given freedom to hug and kiss their dad.

Part of this process is letting them know they are loved regardless of what they look like, how they feel, and how they act. Your love for them is not circumscribed or weakened by anything they do. They can depend on your love unconditionally—you won't ever say, "If you love me, you won't do that."

Of course you'll disagree with their language and actions at times, and you may need to discipline them. But that will not impact the level of your love for them. They desperately need that kind of secure haven, and it permits them to reach out in love and establish relationships with others.

Am I Leading My Child in a Commitment to Growth?

A commitment to growth lets kids know they can make mistakes. It's okay to risk a lot and then blow it, because things will work out.

Mistakes are not always sin; neither is carelessness. They can be opportunities to learn something (even when they happen because of disobedience). Children are eager to try new things and test their skills. It's we parents who sometimes come down hard when kids don't do well, because we think our reputation is at stake.

Teach your children that problems are not catastrophes. They're opportunities for a new and exciting experience. Imagine what a difference that attitude would make when the single mom sees her child perform on the ball field, for example.

Am I Building Consistency into My Child's Life?

Next to unconditional love, the most important thing you can give your children is consistency in what you do.

They need the security of consistency at mealtimes, in what is right and wrong, in the methods of discipline you use, in your expectations of them, and in your own moral life.

A young girl of ten cried as she told her grandmother that she could not understand what was happening to her mom. Her Christian mother had promised her over and over that she would never live with a man. Now, says the daughter, her mother is not only living with another man, but he's not even a Christian. The child is very confused about her mother's spiritual and moral life.

On another matter, one of the most devastating experiences for a child is the parent who regularly says, "You're going to get it for this," but never disciplines the child. Consistent behavior is built into his life when he experiences consistent action on your part as a single mom. Be a person of your word, and he will become a person of his word.

Your expectations of your child may vary significantly from other mothers in your neighborhood. Though that may cause some problems in your children's relationships with other children, if you are consistent in your expectations your child will fall into line and feel secure within the boundaries you have established.

I've known parents who will, for example, be consistent about the kids brushing their teeth during the week, then not pay attention on the weekend. This makes the children wonder why they have to brush their teeth at all. That kind of careless inconsistency can impact other areas, too, such as whether or not to go to church, because that's often the big activity on the weekend.

Being consistent is extremely hard, and no one does it perfectly. But the rewards for your child are well worth your efforts.

Am I Teaching My Child Prompt and Cheerful Obedience to Authority?

Unfortunately, this is not a strong emphasis in our society, so we need to be clear in teaching our children to obey all appropriate authority. It starts with you as a single mom requiring respect from your children. Then it transfers to respect for the school teacher and principal, the Sunday school teacher, pastor, boss. and all other authority figures.

I reemphasize that it is important to teach them to respect *all* authority. In some homes there is respect only for certain people, which may not, for example, include the other parent or the grandparents.

Am I Teaching My Child Self-Discipline?

Early in your child's life, how you model a self-disciplined life will be the most potent factor in determining how self-disciplined your children will become. Self-discipline means passing up immediate gratification for long-term enjoyment.

Self-discipline basically refers to living a controlled life. That may mean your child saves for an eagerly desired toy instead of your simply handing over the money. It may mean sticking with a class in school that he really doesn't like but chose to sign up for. It may mean keeping a promise to help someone else even when it becomes inconvenient later.

Introduce your children to a consistent pattern of reading their Bible and praying. Help them to see that such consistency is not only pleasing to God, but has exciting benefits for them.

Many studies show that how you respond and act is far more important than what you say in helping kids change their behavior and accept your value system.

Am I Teaching My Child to Accept Responsibility?
Your children will be observing how you respond when a specific responsbility is given to you. You may have promised to help the junior high teacher, but a much more exciting opportunity comes along. It's very tempting to change your mind. When you follow through with the teacher, you are showing your child that accepting responsibility for commitments is very important.

Beyond role modeling, help your child to see that keeping a promise even when it hurts is one way of accepting responsibility and building integrity.

Teach your children that tasks you assign to them—such as cleaning up their rooms every Saturday—are important. You may want them to look after their own clothes as they get older, and they'll find a dozen reasons not to do it—unless you insist on it.

The questions I've just listed represent six possible goals you may have for your children. No doubt you'll have some others of your own. Goals are helpful benchmarks for evaluating whether you're "succeeding" as a parent.

But what if your child rebels despite all your best efforts? Does that automatically make you an unsuccessful parent? Not on your life.

WHO'S RESPONSIBLE
FOR HOW THE KIDS TURN OUT?

In an hourglass, all the sand collects on one side until the glass is turned. Then it begins moving into the other side at a very steady rate. At one point there are equal quantities on either side of the narrow neck of the glass. Finally, all the sand passes through the neck to the other side.

When a child is born all the sand is on your side. You have to give them 100 percent, and they are totally under your control. As they grow older they need to take on more and more responsibility for their actions, so that by the time they reach eighteen they're 100 percent responsible for their decisions and actions. During puberty there may be a clash of the wills over how quickly your side of the hourglass should empty, but empty it must.

That being the case, is the parent responsible when an eighteen-year-old rebels against God, parental authority, and society's control? Parents come to me laden with guilt when their child does that, so I ask them, "If your child were to turn out okay, how much of the success would you claim as yours? Give me a specific percentage. Is it 30 percent, 40 percent, 70 percent your responsibility?" The parent will invariably say, "Maybe half a percent, at best one percent is my doing." So I say, "Hold that number."

Then I'll continue, "Now suppose your child is a convicted murderer about to die on death row. How much responsibility do you think you have for that failure?"

Invariably they will peg their responsibility for that child's present condition at 60 to 70 percent. I have to explain, "You have no more right to take responsibility for failure than you do for success." Those numbers have to be the same. But that's a hard thing for any parent to accept.

We must accept that we alone are responsible for our relationship with God—and so are our children. You cannot live off your father's relationship. You cannot acquire a spiritual relationship as an inheritance. Everyone has to respond to God as an individual. And the individual is responsible to God, and no one else.

I'm very aware that the Bible says you can train up

a child in the way he should go, and when he is old he will not depart from it (Proverbs 22:6). Notice the phrase "when he is old." I have a novel interpretation for this phrase. We have to wait until the child is "older" because he will normally—because of his sin nature—not do it when he is young. I didn't do it when I was young. My kids aren't doing it either. But when they're older, I believe they'll be okay. I'm not condoning disobedience, just preparing myself to face reality over my kids. God had much this same situation with the children of Israel.

Between now and getting old is a long time, but you have to wait until they get old. I define old as eighty-three and over.

I cannot emphasize it enough: *Once children reach their late teens and are legally "on their own," they're responsible for their own actions.* God has given them, as a part of creation, the knowledge of good and evil. And that makes them accountable before God for their own actions, no matter what happens.

Psychology has done us a tremendous disservice in focusing too much on the wrong word. We get hung up on asking *why, why, why?* Another word needs to capture more of our attention: it's the word *what*—as in *what are you doing?* Not *why* are you doing it, but *what* are you doing? God wants to know what you have done. He knows the why because we are conceived in sin. But the issue is what we are doing about it—and that is what He will hold us accountable for.

Regardless of how we were raised, there comes a point in time when our parents are off the hook. We become responsible for how we personally respond to the grace of God, and to the moving of His Holy Spirit in our own life.

The best assurance you can have when your child

leaves home is that you did the best you could with the resources you had at the time. You can never go back in time to relive your experiences, but I constantly find single parents stumbling backward into the future. They move ten paces ahead in life and then look at a situation they're in and say, "If I knew then what I know now, how much better I would have been as a parent." They beat themselves to death with "If only I. . . ."

You can't take your new knowledge as a result of life experiences backward into time. Frankly, even I would have been a much better parent if I had known twenty years ago what I know now—but I didn't know it! And I shouldn't condemn myself for that.

A FINAL BENCHMARK: REACHING OUT

There's one final benchmark of progress I want to share with you. When you begin to have concern for others' needs, you've made it around the corner and are on your way to the top.

For example, when you reach out to other single moms who are worse off than you are, then you have successfully negotiated through some of life's worst rapids and reached the calmer waters downstream.

It's very hard to calculate emotional progress, and maturity is tough to define and measure. Certainly spirituality is also tough to measure. These are process issues you will be working at all your life. But you can look at them sideways: that is, you can see the amount of spiritual progress by the level of emotional control you have. If you have a solid relationship with God you will be entering into good relationships with people. Loving others will not crack the surface level without spiritual depth, which involves a vital relationship with Jesus Christ.

SUMMARY

As you seek to do more than just survive as a single parent, keep this advice in mind:

*Hormones can come to life at very inopportune
times — be careful.*

Use the benchmarks of stability to help you focus on progress.

Release authority and responsibility to your child.

Are you succeeding? If you're moving forward in the areas I've outlined in this chapter, I'd say yes. Don't be too concerned about the pace, as long as you're making progress. All God expects of us is faithfulness. As you practice SELF on a consistent basis, you *will* achieve stability in your emotional life. You will have established a loving support system, and you will be stabilizing financially.

Our God is a God of hope. Trust in Him completely — it's the only way to live.

May God richly bless you and your family as you strive to serve Him with your whole heart and train up your children in the way they should go.

Bibliography

Blakeslee, Sandra, and Judith Wallerstein. *Second Chances.* New York: Ticknor and Fields, 1989.

Brandt, Patricia, and Dave Jackson. *Just Me and the Kids: A Course for Single Parents.* Elgin, IL: David C. Cook Publishing Co., 1985.

Brubaker, J. K., and J. I. Slaff. *The AIDS Epidemic: How You Can Protect Yourself and Your Family — Why You Must.* New York: Warner Press, 1985.

Burkett, Larry. *The Complete Financial Guide for Single Parents.* Wheaton, IL: Victor Books, 1991.

Bustanoby, André. *Being a Single Parent.* Grand Rapids, MI: Zondervan Publishing House, 1985.

DeFrain, John D., Julie Elmen, and Judy Fricke. *On Our Own: A Single Parent's Survival Guide.* Lexington, MA: Lexington Books, 1987.

Dobson, Fitzhugh. *How to Single Parent.* New York: Harper & Row, 1987.

Dunteman, Dayna. "Divorce Can Affect the Kids for Ages." *San Bernardino Sun.* March 13, 1990.

Galty, Richard H., and David Koulack. *Single Father's*

Handbook: A Guide for Separated and Divorced Fathers. Garden City, NY: Anchor Books, 1979.

Greif, Geoffrey L. *Single Fathers.* Lexington, MS: Lexington Books, 1985.

Keshet, Harry F., and Kristine M. Rosenthal. *Fathers Without Partners: A Study of Fathers and the Family After Marital Separation.* Totowa, NJ: Rowman and Littlefield, 1981.

Knorr, Dandi Daley. *Just One of Me: Confessions of a Less-Than-Perfect Single Parent.* Wheaton, IL: Harold Shaw, 1989.

McCoy, Kathy. *Solo Parenting; Your Essential Guide: How to Find the Balance Between Parenthood and Personhood.* New York: New American Library, 1987.

Pearson, Lynn. *One on the Seesaw: The Ups and Downs of a Single-Parent Family.* New York: Random House, 1988.

Reed, Bobbie. *I Didn't Plan to Be a Single Parent.* St. Louis, MO: Concordia Publishing House, 1981.

Rekers, George Alan, and Judson J. Swihart. *Making Up the Difference: Help for Single Parents with Teenagers.* Grand Rapids, MI: Baker Book House, 1984.

Richmond, Gary. *The Divorce Decision.* Waco, TX: Word, Inc., 1988.

Richmond, Gary. *Successful Single Parenting.* Eugene, OR: Harvest House Publishers, 1990.

Wayman, Anne. *Successful Single Parenting.* Deephaven, MN: Meadowbrook, 1987.

Weber, Ellen. *Single, But Not Alone.* Nashville, TN: Broadman Press, 1990.

Wright, Norman H. *Christian Use of Emotional Power.* Old Tappan, NJ: Fleming H. Revell, 1979.

Notes

CHAPTER ONE—IT'S NOT EASY BEING A SINGLE PARENT

1. Judith Wallerstein and Sandra Blakeslee, *Second Chances: Men, Women and Children a Decade After a Divorce* (New York: Ticknor and Fields, 1990), page 67.
2. Wallerstein and Blakeslee, page 30.
3. Wallerstein and Blakeslee, page 319.
4. As reported in Dayna Dunteman, "Divorce Can Affect the Kids for Ages," *San Bernardino Sun*, March 13, 1990, page D1.

CHAPTER TWO—UNDERSTANDING THE AGONY

1. Eugene McCreary, "Schools for Fearlessness and Freedom," unpublished.
2. Jim Talley, *Too Close, Too Soon* (Nashville, TN: Thomas Nelson, 1982).

CHAPTER FOUR—RESETTING EXPECTATIONS

1. Norman H. Wright, *The Christian Use of Emotional Power* (Old Tappan, NJ: Fleming H. Revell, 1979).

2. Jim Talley, *Reconcilable Differences* (Nashville, TN: Thomas Nelson, 1985).

3. See J. I. Slaff and J. K. Brubaker, *The AIDS Epidemic: How You Can Protect Yourself and Your Family — Why You Must* (New York: Warner Books, 1985), pages 173-174.

CHAPTER FIVE—RECOGNIZING THE SPECIAL NEEDS OF YOUR CHILDREN

1. Terri S. Speicher, "A Father to the Fatherless," *Focus on the Family* magazine, February 1990, pages 6-7.

2. Adapted from Myrle Carner, "Seven Things Kids Are Dying to Tell Their Parents," *The Christian Leader*, March 13, 1990.

3. Ross Campbell, *How to Really Love Your Child* (Wheaton, IL: Victor Books, 1982) and *How to Really Love Your Teenager* (Wheaton, IL: Victor Books, 1984).

CHAPTER ELEVEN—THE "R" WORD CAN BE THE KEY TO RECOVERY

1. Gary Richmond, *The Divorce Decision: The High Cost of Divorce* (Waco, TX: Word, Inc., 1988).

CHAPTER TWELVE—REMARRIAGE: READY, SET . . . WAIT A MINUTE!

1. Jim Talley, *Reconcilable Differences* (Nashville, TN: Thomas Nelson, 1985).

Authors

Jim Talley has been the Associate Minister of Single Adults at the First Baptist Church in Modesto, California, since 1976. Jim has a Ph.D. in counseling and is a frequent conference speaker. He is the author of seven books and has appeared nationally on "CNN Friday Night Live" as well as "Focus on the Family" with Dr. James Dobson.

Married to Joyce in 1961, the Talleys have three children and four grandchildren. Ordained to the ministry in 1971, Jim has counseled with over 10,000 individuals, most of whom have suffered a broken relationship. The material in his books and seminars is field-tested and has a proven track record of success in the lives of people.

Jim particularly enjoys training lay leaders to do the work of the ministry.

Leslie H. Stobbe is the president of Here's Life Publishers. He has written more than 500 articles and is the author or coauthor of several books, including *Reconcilable Differences* with Jim Talley.